Essays on the Path to Self Discovery Volume II

Introduction

The essays in this collection were written between 2007 and 2010.

The author wishes to share her own experiences and musings on the journey to Self discovery.

The first collection of essays was published together with short stories and practical exercises.

I honor your path knowing that everyone's path to Self discovery is unique.

We are all connected to each other and we are all traveling together in this journey, whether we realize it or not.

Melinda M. Sörensson

Prologue

In Search of Meaning
Man, 1978

What am I?
Man.
In the image of God, breathing.
What am I here for?
I know not.
I search and yet I'm afraid.
If I find my meaning, will I still
live?
Perhaps not.
But the search must
go on.

Table of Contents

Dancing the Dance of Illusion

"We live in illusion, and the appearance of things. There is a reality, we are that reality. When you understand this, you see that you are nothing and being nothing, you are everything. That is all."~Kalu Rinpoche

Even now, I am still guilty of living too much in my mind and of taking everything so seriously all the time. I have always been this way so when I was little I did not spend much time outside of our home.

I spent time with my mother writing on the walls of our home and with my father tending to the farm.

The kids did not like me. I was too serious for them. I took everything that I did seriously, including all the games of softball, scrabble, tag. It was not fun for them

I was into learning everything, so when I was in high school, I actually offered to work at my grandfather's sugarcane fields. His foreman would not allow it and I told him I wouldn't tell my grandfather.

I wanted to experience what it was like for the laborers to cut sugarcane while being fully covered with only eyes showing, in 90 degree Fahrenheit heat and very humid conditions.

One had to be fully covered as the sugarcane has very sharp leaves. In this experiment, I lasted three hours, and my grandfather's foreman paid at the end of the day.

That day I learned the value of manual labor.

In high school the only thing I participated in was dancing and writing for the school paper. Other than that, I went to school, took care of my self and prepared to go to college.

It was the best time of my life.

I had no responsibilities other than my dance, my homework, writing for the school paper, and participating in the weekly clean up in my grandfather's home.

My duty was buffing the massive mahogany staircase and once in a while, washing the dishes. It was heaven.

Pain is teacher. In college, I had to learn what pain was about. The pain of losing my father months before I was to graduate from college.

I do not know if all the wiser, but I survived. I lived my life the same as before. I took everything seriously, and then came intense pain that propelled me to seek what it all means to be in this life, on this earth, with other people.

In 1995,my mother passed away and for the first time I felt alone.

While our relationship had always been strained, in my heart I knew that she was a woman whose wisdom is far from my reach so I almost always did what she told me to do.

I had direction, no matter if I am living in Hawaii or California or Pennsylvania or in Connecticut. Our letters kept us connected.

Her death was a signal that it was time to learn about life on my own.

I was in my late 30s and felt like the 12 year old who left home to live with my grandparents during the week so I can go to a good school and who saw my parents only during the weekends.

The difference is that there are no weekends anymore to look forward to .

I then came upon the writings of Ram Dass, Shunryu Suzuki and Chogyam Trungpa. Even my approach to spirituality was serious.

It is only now that I am able to see myself as I was, so serious on everything, so serious that it is funny, especially when I read the following "Outside of getting out of the paranoid activities your mind, there is no enlightenment per se."~ Chogyam Trungpa

Huh? What about the hours and hours I spent sitting and the hundreds of books I read and all the things I had to give up on this path? You get the point. I was still credential oriented.

It is only now that I can dance the dance of illusion and laugh and cry and experience it all, to the fullest.

As I fed the dogs in the afternoon I realized they will not have any food the following day and immediately my mind went into a frenzy of strategies on how to acquire food for the dogs for tomorrow.

All of a sudden it dawned on me that I was the one who was hungry. I had a wonderful lunch with a dear friend whom I have not seen for a long time so my stomach was full, and yet, I felt hungry.

My son is beginning his adolescent years and prefers to be with his friends and I feel a little bit of abandonment. I was hungry for attention from all of my other friends, and I was hungry for attention from the media about my book.

This is what pure desire feels like. The desire for my son's company,the desire for fame, perhaps. I can make my son spend time with me; all I have to do is ask. There are many ways to get media attention. I know that and yet, deep within is a hunger for the visible manifestation of love.

Observing the feelings, I realized that there is nothing unusual about my feelings. I am human and thus share the desires of everyone else. We all want attention, affection, admiration even. To desire beyond the physical needs is human and I gladly share it with everyone else around me. I realize that yes every once in a while I forget and then, thankfully, remember,that I too chose to dance this dance of illusion and I am happy that I did. I am happy that I do.

I asked my son to go to the supermarket with me to pick up dog food. Being the Bodhisattva that he is, he came without much argument.

We watched the sunset from the front window of a car being driven by an old woman as we took our time to get to the supermarket to fetch dog food. He stayed in the car and I took my time to get other necessities and I was happy to have help loading and unloading the car.

The dogs were happy to see both of us, I think, or maybe they saw the big bag of food on the previously empty space that they see as the source of their meal, but what does it matter? We are all happy to be together here and now.

Life is great. Just to be alive is a gift.

So my advice to everyone is : go ahead, take the risks you would not take otherwise, go where you would not otherwise go, eat foods that you thought you never liked .

Have fun, laugh at yourself more often and dance this dance of illusion.

Today Is a Gift

When I woke up this morning, I was feeling unusually light. After taking my son to school and feeding Hershey and Blair my "daughters", I proceeded to cook my son's lunch.

At 10:30 am, I had already de-cluttered the house, done one load of laundry, and tidied up my son's room. I think he still thinks that a fairy waves her magic wand when he leaves in the morning so that his room is spic and span when he comes home.

I am sure we have already heard it before, from the sages before us, even from our parents, that every day we are alive is a gift. Today, I realized how truly fortunate I am to be living in this lifetime, sharing lives with everyone around me, including the birds that take baths in our backyard fountain and then fly away.

In one single day, so many things happen all at once, and we are both part of it and at the center of it-for everything that we see on the outside happens on the inside first. It is a great day to be alive.

Cleaning the Cobwebs of My Mind

I can't remember a day in my life that I didn't clean the house I am in. I clean when I am happy, I clean when I am sad. I clean when I am relaxed, I clean when I am tense, I clean when I am tired and I clean when I am just hanging out.

I tell myself that there is no one who will do a better job than I do, and yet I am perfectly happy when other people clean our other properties. I tell myself that I am particular about who comes and goes in my house and yet it is open to everyone I know. So many excuses not to have someone clean for me.

The house we live in is just like any other lived in house. It is alive, with dust and dogs hair everywhere. There are un-shelved dvds and un-boxed VCR tapes. And yet I clean every day. I think I am trying to rearrange my surroundings when it is my mind that is chaotic. Cleaning is my crutch.

Perhaps, I am trying to clean the cobwebs in my mind, and perhaps, someday, I will look around and there will be nothing more to clean.

But not today.

While Scrubbing the Bathroom Floor

Sitting meditation is a gift I give myself. My logical mind says there is no time to meditate since there is so much work to be done.

Cleaning is one of the things that I enjoy and every once in a while, in moments when I am absorbed in what I am doing, I have a glimpse of our interconnectedness with all that the eyes can see, all that there ever is, or was, our ignorance, the truth about suffering and the cause of suffering.

I have now realized that there are several things I am obsessed about: Constant cleaning, indicative of the inherent disorder in my mind, constant worrying about money, an insecurity, constant fear of the future that prevents me from enjoying the present, the now, the only truth and the only reality.

What I must do instead is to accept the present, enjoy it to the fullest because there is only now.

In this life, if we realize that our life is finite in this body, and yet eternal, for the spirit, the soul, the light, the essence, IT (as Alan Watts calls it) always comes back until we have reached perfection in which case we no longer have to come back. Our existence in this lifetime is nothing but a school. The school of life, where every encounter is a lesson, every moment is a lesson, then magically, our worries diminish, our fears fade, not completely, but our anger, our greed, the game of one-upmanship is reduced to a lesson and when we suffer, we can accept the suffering and let it pass.

We look at the past and we say "Oh, so much energy wasted." It is wasted energy only to the extent that we regret. But what do we regret? Why do we regret? We think.

 We believe that we could have done something else, but if only our judging minds will give up and realize that every moment is perfection in motion then there will be a space between the judging and the events and we will realize that we always did what we could do at the time.

Even this moment that I am scrubbing the bathroom floor and the phone is ringing off the hook.

I wish that in this moment, my son would appreciate our black lab more, walk her more, pet her more. While I expect it of him it is I who has not done any of that today.

I have been so selfish ...I think only in terms of I, I, I, me, me, me. I am busy thinking of myself and how things affect me!

Oh, I am the one who should develop compassion...I pray with all of my heart that my heart be pure, that my mind be rid of all these clutter, that I am able to see things differently instead of being confined to this I that was created by my ego.

Vanishing Significances

My girlfriend whom I have been friends with for over thirty years sends me a present every year for Christmas and birthdays.

For many years after my divorce she has sent me the most beautiful lingerie from Victoria's Secret, wishing I would somehow use them. But I am a very practical person and either gave them away to other friends or donated them to Salvation Army so that at least someone can use them.

She got tired of sending me those lovely womanly things because when she asked, "Have you used the latest one I sent you?" The answer was always the same. "I gave it away to someone who would actually use them." I have had no need for them.

If there Is one thing one can count on me for, it is that I will always tell the truth at that moment one asks, but the people who ask are also aware that those can change.

For example, I may not be hungry now, but I could be later or vice versa. It makes things very simple. I live in moment to moment truths.

This year she sent me a whole set of skin care and the instructions on how to use them. She is a chemist, used only to the best and so I actually read everything she wrote on the separate card and will summarize them here.

The specific products you can ask me if you are interested. Here are the instructions :

1. Use sunscreen. The higher the SPF, the better. Never leave home without it.
2. Use the body skin firming cream. This I do not need to do, I think.
3. Use vanishing cream at night to get rid of the age spots. I must admit this I have to use. One of the costs of being pregnant is the change in the hormones and we get more susceptible to sun damage. It is a fact.
4. Use eye cream to get rid of puffy eyes.
5. Eat well. Drink lots of water.
The vanishing cream is imported. I will not write it here. The major component is hydroquinone. The scientific name of it is Benzene-1,4-diol or quinol, is an aromatic organic compound that is a type of phenol, having the chemical formula $C_6H_4(OH)_2$.

I came to think about that word, vanishing.

To vanish according to Merriam Webster online means this :
intransitive verb
1 a : to pass quickly from sight : disappear
b : to pass completely from existence

2: to assume the value zero
transitive verb
: to cause to disappear
— van·ish·er noun

Examples of VANISH

1. The missing girl vanished without a trace a year ago.
2. The papers seem to have vanished into thin air .
3. Dinosaurs vanished from the face of the earth millions of years ago.
Origin of VANISH
Middle English vanisshen, from Anglo-French vaniss -, stem of vanir, envanir, esvanir, from Vulgar Latin *exvanire, alteration of Latin evanescere to dissipate like vapor, vanish, from e- + vanescere to vanish, from vanus empty
First Known Use: 14th century
Related to VANISH
Synonyms: dematerialize, dissolve, evanesce, evaporate,fade, flee, fly, go (away), melt, sink, disappear

Antonyms: appear, materialize

Hydroquinone will lighten the age spots. Four percent hydroquinone applied consistently is supposed to vanish all the age spots. The purpose of the vanishing cream is to lighten unnecessary dark spots or discolorations on the skin. In mine, the only ones I have are those areas that are constantly exposed to the sun. The face. One can see them on my picture. I do not use make up and I have thrown away make up sets.

There is a caveat when one uses this, it is imperative that the skin never be exposed to the UV rays without sunscreen. The sunscreen actually has to be applied an hour before going out into the sun. Where I live, there is always sun, even if it does get cold.

I thought about the vanishing effects. When one takes away the awareness of something, anything, then the importance of it vanishes. It actually disappears. It is very tricky and it will take a while before one realizes this but when one is aware one can prove it experientially, and then a whole new world opens.

To vanish the significance of something, anything, one has to be able to go into it, be it, then view it from another perspective. Try it with something right in front of you. Anything will do. A pen, a rock, a quarter. It does not matter what. When I was doing it as part of the course, it took me half a day to do the exercise, to be good at it so above all else be patient with yourself and don't push. The trick really is to do it effortlessly. This will take time and lots and lots of practice. When you get really good at it, you will find that it will be very difficult to get upset, because you can vanish the significance of anything, at will.

I used the cream so that I can tell my friend that I am actually using the presents she sent. There was considerable change, overnight. This is theoretically impossible, but perhaps, I willed it to be so, so that I can validate to her that her system works.

She is fifty and looks thirty five. Magic.

Absolute Power

This is an answer to one of the posts in the hubpages comments on the article The Six Kinds of Power.

The body is a shell. It does have cellular memory. We need it to be in this world, on this planet, in this galaxy.

The mind is like a fly which alighted on a giant's shoulder and thinks itself to be master, but it is largely a programmed mass of imprints...this is sad but it is true.

The spirit, the breath of God, is what animates the body, but in most of us, it is asleep.

The mind therefore thinking that it can command the body makes it a slave to the demands of the body and to its own demands...and it has endless demands...we see this when we meditate and see that thoughts arise one after another.

It says me me me...me first, me only, serve me.

The spirit or soul is perfect but it is sleeping and needs to reawaken in order to assert itself.

When it has awakened, it sees the cruelty of the mind.

Awake, it sees itself as it really is. Boundless compassion, unlimited and unconditional love, more powerful than what the mind can conceive itself to be, no matter how grandiose the vision.

An awakened spirit knows itself to be eternal, invincible and invulnerable, but to get to that stage there are tests after tests after tests.

Absolute power can corrupt in human terms but one is never given absolute power unless firstly it has developed panoramic awareness which does not allow it to be frivolous in any sense.

In the Buddhist tradition, it makes one lift the cockroach off the floor and take it outside so it can live. In the Christian tradition, it is the story of a saint getting the scissors and cutting off an expensive veil to half when she needed it, because a cat was sleeping on the other half.

In the Bhagavad Gita, it is Krishna's answer to Arjuna's decrying his having to fight his cousins in the war.

The temptation of Jesus Christ literally sums it all up.

That was the koan, a riddle, which one could understand intellectually and from the heart but to understand and relate to is different than to know.

The Tangled Web of Our Desires

I am a compulsive cleaner. It is for me an escape, an expression of a desire to change my surroundings as a reflection of the desire to change something inside and this happens quite a bit.

When we examine our desires, we see that they arise from nowhere and yet it seems to have a life of their own.

For example in the case of cleaning, I would first notice the clutter and want to get rid of it so that in my line of sight,there is only simplicity and thus beauty, but then, I would also begin to notice that the toilet needs scrubbing and the floor needs mopping, and on and on.

I would then begin to rearrange the clothes in the closet and before I know it, I am doing three loads of laundry just because I wanted to declutter.

If we have a desire for food, the desire is not satisfied by eating the food that we thought of first. It is followed by a desire for another and then another.

If we have a desire for a large amount of money, that desire is also followed by a desire on what to spend the money on. And so it goes on and on and on.

The desire does not have to be confined to the material level. It can be spiritual as well. When we want to help someone, then we want to help because we think that what we do will make them happy and in turn it will make us happy. Thus the karmic wheel goes on.

If we examine our desire, in all honesty, we can catch a glimpse of the space within which that desire emanates and surely we will see that there is a gap. It is this gap that we have to be in, in order to get out of our karmic bondage.

When we see that our cleaning is an escape, or that the desire for more food when we are already full is really an expression of a deeper longing for something else, or that when we give anything there does not have to be an attachment to it, we enter that gap.

In that gap is freedom.

I Said Goodbye to Yesterday

My son is still sleeping. This week he moves into the dormitories to begin his new life as a college freshman.

The garbage truck was late today. They normally come at 6:30 am, but they came five hours later. I watched as the giant arms of the truck grabbed the massive trash bin which can hold, if it were disassembled, and without the engine of the car, a whole car.

I watched as part of my life got lifted and thrown together with the trash of a whole neighborhood, remnants of what I held dear, a part of me.

Old photographs, old letters, I have been hanging on to them for so long they have traveled all the way from Honolulu to California to Pennsylvania to Connecticut and here to Louisiana, over a span of 18 years. It is time to let go of what once was, but it was not so easy.

I agonized about throwing a lot of it away. I feel like I should have created a big bonfire to celebrate freedom from the past but it is just another drama.

I said goodbye to the dramas in my life as well. I created them all and I can create them again. For now, I am not being, not doing, and not having or is it the other way around?

Tomorrow I go back to what I first loved. But that is tomorrow. Just for today I will celebrate.

Catharsis, Metamorphosis and Stasis, the Way of the Bodhisattva

I read Chogyam Trungpa's work when I started meditation. My copy of his book, "The Myth of Freedom" is falling apart at the seams. I have used it again and again.

In the beginning, it was too esoteric for me. It appealed to my intellect. As the years went on and I continued the discipline he so much adhered to, I began to see the truth in what he had written, experientially.

It was awe inspiring and frightening at the same time.

He had talked about the Prajnaparamita close to the end of the book.

In the Heart Sutra it says: "Therefore the mantra of transcendent knowledge, the mantra of deep insight, the unsurpassed mantra, the incomparable mantra, the mantra that calms all suffering should be known as Truth, for there is no deception.

In transcendent knowledge the mantra is proclaimed: Om Gate Gate Paragate Parasamgate Bodhi Svaha"

In English the rendering of the mantra is Gone, Gone, Gone Beyond, Completely Gone Beyond,enlightenment, Hail
In each and everyone's life there is a series of catharsis. A spiritual cleansing, if you will. We do this at will when we sit and meditate, whether we like it or not. Discipline.

The Merriam Webster online dictionary defines catharsis as

Definition of CATHARSIS
1: purgation
2a : purification or purgation of the emotions (as pity and fear) primarily through art
b : a purification or purgation that brings about spiritual renewal or release from tension

3: elimination of a complex by bringing it to consciousness and affording it expression

Meditation is like washing clothes, or extracting something in the laboratory.

You take off layer after layer of dust from the mind,or from the clothes, and in case of isolating something in the laboratory, you take more and more of the material stripping it off of the source and the more your product you recover.

In the case of washing, the greater number of times you do it, the cleaner the clothes become. It is empirically so.

Meditation is an active process and the truths you encounter are solely your own.

Metamorphosis is never ending. It is a continuous process until death and the ensuing return.

I do not want to use rebirth for personal reasons. A consequence of catharsis is the continuous removal of occlusions. Our blind spots.

We arrive at truths one truth at a time.

The definitions of metamorphosis:

1a : change of physical form, structure, or substance especially by supernatural means

b : a striking alteration in appearance, character, or circumstances
2: a typically marked and more or less abrupt developmental change in the form or structure of an animal (as a butterfly or a frog) occurring subsequent to birth or hatching

Finally, stasis. Where everything is held as an unlimited potential. It is what is in between thoughts.

Definitions of STASIS

1: a slowing or stoppage of the normal flow of a bodily fluid or semifluid: as

a : slowing of the current of circulating blood
b : reduced motility of the intestines with retention of feces

2a : a state of static balance or equilibrium : stagnation

b : a state or period of stability during which little or no evolutionary change in a lineage occurs

The cocoon is symbolic in the sense that it holds the potential for a butterfly. So is a seed.

For a bodhisattva, the stasis can be eons. He can, at will, emerge,and engage in compassionate action, not necessarily as a butterfly.

Being human is where he can help the most.

A true warrior does not have to engage in war all the time.

Choose Peace, Moment by Moment

Time and time again, the sages have told us that we only have now. Everything that we do is in the now. This is true of everything.

Awareness requires choice, a moment by moment decision. Do we mutter obscenities because a driver cut right in front of us? Do we yell at our kids for leaving the dirty clothes on the floor instead of the hamper?

Do we get mad at our dogs for still using the living room as a toilet? Our programming keeps us hooked in these mini traps, day in and day out.

This is probably one of the reasons why sannyasins minimize contact with the outside world as long as possible so they can work on themselves.

Yes, they do come back into the world when they have done all the work and then come back when they can no longer be sidetracked. They have arrived.

Few of us can take the leap of leaving our families behind to go deep in the mountains and work on ourselves.

We have to do that in addition to taking care of our families, creating the money for our necessities and for the few luxuries that we deem necessary, in this period of our lives.

As long as we are part of this society, being in our dharma, we will have to deal with dirty laundry, other drivers, our pets, our workers, our bosses, our financial planners and insurance agents, but it all makes a beautiful tapestry.

We simply have to look and find the beauty and simplicity of it all.

In my mind, the words beauty, simplicity and perfection are synonymous. Even the most complicated mandalas, with their variegated colors and patterns show simplicity. How do we see this simplicity in our day to day encounters with everyone around us?

Only our minds create a tangled web and pushes us into confusion.

Our ego says that our annoyance and even our anger is righteous. Yet we can look at everything in our lives as simple as a karmic necessity.

The enlightened ones never even think about these happenings as a karmic necessity.

They choose peace, moment by moment.

Conscious Awareness of Who You Are

"You are what your deep driving desire is. As your desire, so is your will, as your will, so is your thought, as your thought, so is your deed, as your deed so is your destiny"-Brihadaranyaka Upanishad

Tonight I am thinking of three words.
Perfection in Motion.

Each and every individual life is perfection in motion and as soon as we accept this, the more space we have with with to work. It is the meaning of being in the NOW.

We see that as each moment unfolds, there is a freshness, openness, a wide open space.

It was all perfection in motion which I am now able to see from a distance.

We have this choice. Moment to moment we can accept this moment as full, perfect and complete in and by itself.

I urge you to look at your own life right NOW and see where your discomfort is.

You will see that it is springing from something that you think as imperfection, when the easiest thing to do is to ACCEPT this moment as it is.

Pay attention to your breath. Where did your thought and worry go? This is awareness. With it comes peace, and with peace comes power.

Paradoxical but true nevertheless.

I wish you moment to moment peace. You have this power to choose what to focus on at every moment. Take it.

Focus on the good, the beautiful and the sublime. It is who you are. You have simply forgotten. Take the time to remember it with every breath you take, consciously.

Fear as a Vehicle for Freedom

If we look at the times when we were most afraid, truly, we would see that our fear did not have any value at all. All it did was to create a temporary imbalance in our thinking process, a hardness of muscle at the back of our heads, and a pain in the stomach.

I know I have been there many times. To take a leap into the unknown is not for the faint at heart.

I was fearless before my son was born. I had always been independent as a child, always decided for myself and did things my own way. My independence was a product of the unconditional love that my parents surrounded us with when we were children.

There was nothing I could do to make them "not love me anymore." I had gone through life forging ahead and at times just hanging out, but the only person that I had to take care of was I, and I knew I would manage. And I did manage well.

And then my son came along. He chose to be born to me. All of a sudden I had to take care of someone else. The game changed. It was when I learned of fear.

I can remember that when he was little, I would go look at him when he was sleeping and then when I did not notice any movement, I would put my head on his tiny chest and then really listen to see if his heart was beating, for he slept so quietly. This was paranoia, for I read all of the books and he was healthy and I gave up all the things that I enjoyed when I learned that I was pregnant. For the first time in my life, I knew what fear was. Fear of not having enough money, fear of not doing a good job raising him, fear of not being able to provide for his future, fear of the values that I would instill in him as a human being, and on and on and on. Endless fear. But that was then. I look at it now as a memory that I could always bring back to the present if I choose to, but the NOW is much more fascinating than the past.

In the distant past, there were two times that I could have died in an accident, and I didn't. I miraculously survived! When I let go, it was fine. I was fine. Those were the times that I let go of all of the things I defined myself to be and just said "God, if it is Thy Will, so let it be done". And in those times were inexplicable flashes of consciousness that I am not able to write about because I really do not know how. I do know that at those times, my faith was perfect, unclouded by the chatter of my logical mind, albeit momentarily.

Faith is the absence of fear and this is what is beautifully illustrated by Psalm 23.

I have read the bible many times. First I concentrated on the old testament and I always went back to the story of David, and I kept wondering why Steven Spielberg has not yet made a movie about David. He was so human!

What Moses, and David and all the great figures in the bible had was faith. What Buddha had on his journey to awakening was faith. It requires perfection. A moment to moment decision to let go. It does not come without a price. To let go of something we hang on to requires fearlessness in facing the unknown, jumping into the abyss.

To some, it has to begin with courage, the ability to face your fears when they arise. One fear at a time. Fear is of the future.

We almost always fear something that might happen in the future that we forget about the now, the never-ending now. Face your fears now and make a decision to remember that fear is what you think tomorrow or next week or next ten years will be. What about now?

What will you do about the situation you are so afraid of that will happen at some other arbitrary time in the future? We only have NOW and when we truly realize that, there is no longer room for fear. Choose to live life NOW.

Feelings as Gateways or Suffering as a Choice

English is my second language. Although I have been living in America for more than half of my life, I will never fully understand all of the jokes and the idioms that I come across. I suppose that I can make that a reason for not being able to express everything that I feel in words, but there are times when words simply can not capture the meaning.

Absolute happiness, perfect clarity, and immeasurable grief are descriptions and yet we can not fully grasp the meaning of those unless we have been there.

We have to have experienced what they describe in order to relate to the phrases. They all connote intense feelings, and as long as we are alive we will have human feelings.

The common thread in all of these phrases is their relation to love. In this way, I mean love as a connection to the source and therefore no distinction between the different kinds of love as we call them.

We all come from a place of love. No matter the circumstances of our birth as we know it in this lifetime, no matter how hard our life had been, we sometimes experience moments of intense clarity and moments of sublime peace. It is in those moments when we embody love-universal love.

We don't have to seek love outside of ourselves.

We are love and therefore have perfect connection to everything and everyone around us.

When we suffer, we are disconnected from that which we really are. It is in those times that we have to make the choice. We can either choose to be grateful for our lives, or we can choose to suffer. No matter what we choose, we can always turn to something that will bring us out of it.

Feelings remind us of our humanity. Even Jesus wept.

The Buddha suffered pain when he left his wife and child. Arjuna was anguished because he had to face in battle some people whom he dearly loved.

King David fully embodied the gamut of all human feelings. They are our examples. We honor our feelings because they will always be a part of us. We acknowledge them because they remind us of our humanity and then we let them go.

Happy or sad we have to remember that everything changes, and yes, no matter how much we try to hang on to them, they too shall pass, and we renew ourselves moment by moment.

How to Possess the Key to Everything

I am an auditory learner. I grew up on a farm in rural Philippines and we only had radios. There was no electricity. I can remember listening to "The Voice of America" and a show called "The Heart is a Lonely Hunter" I was too young to relate to the romantic side of it, but I loved the music.

I know it is by one of the classical composers but who it is escapes me right now.
The heart, truly is a lonely hunter. To hunt is not it's function.

Its function is to give freely, without bounds and without expectations. Its function is to love unconditionally.

Unconditional love is the key to everything: every material desire, every relationship desire, literally, everything. To arrive there one must work a lot.on oneself.

To arrive at that space we have to let go of all our egoistic identifications. We can pray, meditate, do yoga, the only object of which is to arrive at a perfect union with the Divine.

There is no other way. Literally and figuratively it is the key to everything.

The heart is at the center of chakras whether coming up or down from the base to the seventh chakra. It is possible to open the third eye by using mantras. It is where all the psychic powers can be had, and yet, when the heart is not open then we are still on child's play, fulfilling egoistic needs with our psychic powers.

Nobody wants to block the heart consciously, and yet every time our egos get pricked and we respond to it , it is a heart blockage. We need to release everything.

In the past six weeks, I have been only "Listening to My Heart."

To get there I had to relate to the intense pain of looking within. While in deep meditations over many years, I experienced involuntary tears coming from my eyes a great number of times. I know this is a form of release for all of the pains I either dismissed or refused to acknowledge and all of my unconscious attachments. The tears no longer came after a certain point and I thought, wow, I have graduated from my attachments, finally! I was wrong!

I am a trained scientist and as such trained to only believe what I see, in the form of experiments. Even going through the process of looking within and recognizing where the pain was coming from, I had to look as an observer and look at the experiences with that training. Intense suffering is real, but it is intelligent.

I can, at will, dismiss all of if by exhausting everything with the question "Why?" but that would be putting a bandaid over a very deep gash, and in the long run it would not work. We ALL have to go to the roots of our suffering. It is the first Noble truth. Suffering springs from attachment. All attachments.

This time, when I cried during meditations, I KNEW why I was crying.

To relate to the ego we must work on ourselves via meditation or contemplation or prayer. Do what you think is best for you at the moment and then move on when it is necessary. We honor our paths.

Because I have been a student of spirituality for a long time, I can, at will, go into the Space of Unconditional Love with people I love. I call it a Sacred Space.

When I said at will it is because I choose to do so. Choosing is still ego's function. This is not what I am talking about. I am talking about being open hearted at times when it is difficult. The ego is so intelligent it can use everything to assert itself and lull us into THINKING we are free. The real test now comes from the heart. Are you able to trust your heart?

I do not recommend that you follow your instincts all the time. It is only at times when there is a conflict between logic and what your heart tells you that you follow your heart. Trust yourself. Trust your feelings. I will always remember the scene from Star Wars when Luke Skywalker was trying to raise his spaceship from the marshes when he landed on Yoda's planet. He could do it at will for a few minutes and it would sink again. Then Yoda said "Trust your feelings, Luke"

I mentioned this because it required that:

1. Luke trusted Yoda
2. Luke did not ask Yoda to do it for him! He could have, just as Peter did when he was sinking whereas before he was walking on water, and he told Jesus Christ, "Lord, I am sinking" at which time Jesus Christ extended a hand.

3. When Luke finally trusted himself , fully, Yoda raised his spaceship from the marshes and off he went. He was finally a Jedi Knight.

Not yet a Master. That test was when he faced Darth Vader and left himself completely at the mercy of Darth Vader during the final battle between him and his father.

He was vulnerable yet he knew that that was what was needed to be done. In that act, Luke liberated Darth Vader.

To trust the heart? Completely? At first, no. Fear will be everywhere. Your ego will keep on saying "What are you doing? Why are you doing this? Are you crazy?" .Fear is the ego's way to project something in the future based on the past. A projection into the future from the memory of a past. Acknowledge that voice and give it a pat. Your ego is a friend, not an enemy.

How to get there? By the choices that we make, moment to moment, this is awareness.

By contemplating on the heart while meditating, by praying for others, by forgiving, continuously, the perceived slights that we encounter day after day, and the most important, letting go of the past.

No matter how glorious or how sad it was, it is in the past. Let it go.

In Simplicity Lies Beauty

Truths are very simple. They are our reminders that we can not go on creating romantic delusions about anything.

Beauty never lies. One sees it and is immediately touched by it. Yet the beauty of the flower, a fresh flower, and one's appreciation of it lies deeper than meets the eye.

For it is the heart that is touched, the divine in us when we see beauty.

Of the artworks, I like the simple paintings of the Masters. In them lie true beauty. Our minds are so complicated.

When we are able to see a thought arise and vanish, on its own, we see that everything is simple.

We are the only ones who complicate it, not necessarily through our own doing but because we are accustomed to it. In order to be, we have to undo past habits, conditioning.

When we examine, truly examine beautiful things, we find that they are quite simple and that the complexities are only created in our minds by our minds. To see things as they are is the ultimate form of simplicity but this is not quite as easy as it sounds.

By the time we are ready to understand this, we have already been through so much past conditioning that we have to "undo" in order to "be".

Being is in the now, where everything is reduced to a grain of sand, or a multitude of galaxies or very simply your dogs asking you to fill their water bowls.

From Essence to Quintessence

My son and I share a passion for history. I must admit that as I write this, he knows more about it than I do. I look at history in terms of people, what drives them.

I love old houses. They have character. They are imprinted with the signature of the previous owners. I love the house that we live in. It is perfect for the four of us. My son, my two dogs and myself.

The house that we live in is quite ordinary. It has three bedrooms and two full baths and a half bath outside. I always wondered why there is a bathroom outside of the main house. One of my previous colleagues told me that it was probably constructed for the help who landscaped the yards.

It does have a very big backyard. It took me two years to find this house and it was as perfect then as it is now. I had to change a couple of things here and there, but the yard is pretty much the same except for the addition of a water fountain.

Oh except one of the trees fell off when hurricane Lily passed. On it's stump I placed a concrete statue of the Buddha. This one is unusual because it is a smiling Buddha and the hands are not folded in a meditation posture. It is as if the Buddha is just enjoying the traffic of all kinds of birds taking baths in the fountain, the squirrels that tease the dogs and, one day, even a snake.

All part of the dance of life in my backyard.

The couple who used to live here are retired and they did a terrific job of landscaping the property. Even now, when the azaleas are in bloom, ours is the only home surrounded by magnificent colors in our neighborhood which also an older neighborhood.

I can only remember one house that seems to change owners unusually frequently for as long as we have lived here.

Most of the residents on the houses lining the street are either retired or working at home, so on any one weekday, the cars are parked on the carports as if it were a weekend.

The pine tree in the backyard is the tallest on the street. I can see it as long as I am on the same street. It serves as a beacon to me.

The flowering plants that continue to give us flowers were planted by the previous owners. I am always grateful for the generosity of spirit of the previous owners for leaving us this gift. I can tell they loved the land as I do now.

That is the history of this house for me. That is what I will remember when I either move away someday or die. I wonder how it was for the people who built it? I wonder how my son will remember it when he goes to college? He always thought it too small. No swimming pool. No tennis court. Not a place for big parties. For me, it is perfect. Small enough that I know where he and the dogs are at any one time even when I am at work on my computer.

I will always remember this house as the house where I found the most peace. When I pass on the ownership of this house to someone else, I wonder what they would change and what they would keep? What kind of signature will they leave? I hope that at least they will keep the bananas and the lemon tree and the dogwoods that I planted.

Oh and I will leave them the Buddha on the stump and the water fountain as my gift, just like the previous owners left calla lilies and African daisies and the enormous fig tree as their legacy to the future occupants of the land. For the land remains. The house may change, the occupants do change, but the land will always keep a record of the life that was there.

How to Adjust to Life's Transitions

Life is a flow. Transitions happen whether we like it or not. Impermanence is the nature of everything outside of ourselves. It is not the moments that we label "big" that requires our full attention. It is the moment to moment change.

When we pay attention, there can never be "big" moments.

A samurai lives each moment ready to die at any other moment, either through the hands of his opponent, or his own. In this way, he is fearless, and that is how we should all be.

It is hard to imagine the loss of a loved one through separation or divorce or death. The pain is an indication of attachment.

One wise man told me that all relationships come to an end, either voluntarily or involuntarily. He meant ALL relationships.

When my father died, I cried, but not at his deathbed. I cried at my graduation months later because I knew he would have been proud of me and I wished so much for him to be there.

He had bone cancer and at the very end of his illness, he winced in pain if someone sat on the edge of his bed.

He refused to take any more morphine because he was not lucid when he took it and he wanted to spend whatever remaining hours of his life seeing us and talking to us. I saw his death as the end of his physical and mental pain.

The separation from a person, to whom you have spent a lot of your time with, is painful. There is always a sense of rejection and an endless tirade of questions mostly directed against ourselves. We ask if we could have done something differently and better, but the answer is that we did all we can given what we had.

Our children will grow old and have a life of their own and no matter how much we cling to them as children, we have to also honor their own paths to growth. We also have to accept the fact that our bodies will also grow old and eventually die and decay.

In some Buddhist sects, one of the practices to cease the identification with this body is to look at a decaying corpse and contemplate impermanence.

Leaving a job, voluntarily or involuntarily is not always easy. We somehow identify with what we do and it is fearsome to lose that identity, eventually we realize that we are so much more than what we did.

Transition points are points of change and therefore points of power. The power to choose which direction we would take. If we would only go with the path of least resistance then our choice would be a wise one.

If you are at a point of transition in your life, here are the things that you can do:

Take a day off from everything and everyone. If you have children, arrange for them to be with your friend or a babysitter for the whole day.

Clean your closet and ask yourself, do I love myself when I wear this outfit when I look in the mirror? If the answer is no, donate it to the Salvation Army or Goodwill. It will make you feel good.

Spend a day at the spa. You deserve to be pampered. You deserve to be pampered regardless but especially so now because you are forming a new relationship with yourself.

You will be your own best friend from now on.

Do something or buy something that will symbolize a new beginning. It is up to you. Rearrange furniture. Give away the ones you do not absolutely adore.

Plant a tree. If you do not have a backyard, then use a planter to plant perennials. Go to a shop that you have never been before, not to buy, but to appreciate and admire.

Break out the china and the goblets and make yourself a favorite dinner as if you are having the finest guest you can have in your town. You are the finest guest in town.

Take your car to the car wash or wash it yourself as if it were the car you have always dreamed of having and now you have it. You will appreciate your car more because this time, you will spend time with it.

Try on one of the clothes that you chose to keep and go to the supermarket in them. Why not?

Clear away the clutter on your desk.

Go through your cupboards and remove those gadgets that you bought but only used once or twice.

After the day you spend with yourself, did you like your own company? Now you are ready to go back, but it is really not the same anymore is it?

The house is cleaner, there is more space, you look at yourself in the mirror and you say, hey, not too bad!

You don't have to go through transitions to experience a renewed love for yourself.

Every time you breathe and you pay attention to your breathing, not controlling, but just paying attention, you cultivate it. Try it.

Observing Life While Being In It, Awareness and Detachment

Yesterday I saw a robin in the bush outside my home office, close enough to touch, the only thing separating us from each other being a few feet of space and a screen door.

Last night, the whole world watched as the police interviewed people who had gotten in contact with the gunman at Virginia Tech.

Today, I watched myself hang on to a piece of property that is a symbol of independence and awakening for me, even if it meant I might not close on a substantial deal.

Even I asked myself, "Why?". It is just a piece of land and old worn-down house. And yet it means much to me. Why did a young man take the lives of others and his own? What is it that motivates human beings?

Human beings have an attachment to people, things, places, events, memories, ideas. The attachment is our anchor to who we think we are, our sense of self which is so relative to everyone and everything around us.

It is as if when we let go of the anchor we would float in space and fade away and we are all afraid of that. We might not know who we are anymore. Or we might, and that is even scarier. It is so much easier to just remain in trance. The choice that one character in "The Matrix" took. He did not want to wake up.

The rope that tethers us to the anchor is also the rope that binds us. Our thoughts.

And now I realized what Richard Bach meant when he wrote "Break the chains of your thoughts, and you break the chains of your body too", in Jonathan Livingston Seagull.

Perhaps in that space where we can observe our thoughts we may see that we are so much more, and that ultimately, we are all one.

Our Greatest Gift As a Human Being

If you could rewrite your life, would you? What would it be like? Your thoughts are a double edged sword. They can either imprison you or liberate you and allow you to soar like an eagle.

As long as we live on this planet, in this lifetime, we are bound to honor karmic necessities. By karmic necessities I mean the choices that WE made before we were born to this personality that we now call "me" or "you", which are the roles that we chose to play in this lifetime. First as a son or daughter, then so on and so on.

Our individual roles which are necessary definitions in order to help us learn that we may go back to where we came from, and from there choose to come back or stay.

How does one live a life of balance with so many things pulling us from one direction to another? When you discover your own true Self, you will realize that life on this planet as you experience it is all a grand play. The best part of it is that you are the producer, director, stage manager, and, you also play the lead role in your own life experiences.

As long as we are alive, we can choose how we experience each moment. The power to choose how we feel is our greatest gift as a human being.

You can choose to create the life that you want, and then live it to the fullest.

We only live once in this body and in this lifetime. We ought to make the best of it. And because we can create our own play, why not? Choose your thoughts because they are the prelude to your actions. With your thoughts you can either create a happy life NOW or be imprisoned by your past or be paralyzed by your fear of the future.

Choose well. Choose to be happy NOW, then create the life that you want, first in your imagination, then with your actions. You deserve to live a happy life and you can make that happen.

You simply have to choose to begin where you are. Right HERE and Right NOW.

Paradoxes as Pathways to Freedom or the Art of Letting Be

One of my friends called me a few days ago. It seems that he is not getting as much of the family fortune as one of his siblings is, and this upsets him.

I had to remind him he does not need any more. He is already independently wealthy. I think his point is the unfairness of it all. His reaction is very normal.

Sometimes we equate love with material gifts. We are humans after all. We want to be loved, appreciated, gifted, treated fairly, but who decides what is fair and what is not?

"Let it Be" sang the Beatles. It is my favorite of all their songs, even if I may say, I love all their songs. "Whisper words of wisdom, let it be".

Hanging onto an idea or to something or someone is an attachment that we all feel at one time in our lives.

I remember breaking up with my first love. I thought I was going to die.

I wanted to die. I felt unloved and unwanted. In an ocean of grief and anger and feeling unwanted, I decided to go home to my parents, sleep, be awakened by my mother so that I will have food in my stomach and go back to sleep again, and then miraculously, in one weekend,

I am whole again. I let it go. I survived.

I am reminded of the paradoxes of holding water as you cup your hand, or taking a scoop of sand. If you squeeze your hand in anyway, water comes out, or sand falls. The same is true of everything in life. The more we hang on to things/people/events, the more we find ourselves feeling a loss. At that moment, we choose to suffer. Nobody wants to suffer and yet our conditioned reactions make it our default mode.

The only antidote for any suffering is conscious awareness. We feel the feeling and appreciate it, for it reminds us that we are alive, and then, we choose to let go. We choose to let it be. In the moment that we truly let go,when we are no longer part of the drama but a mere observer, we see the space with which we can create and life begins again.

Yes, we begin life moment by moment. So whatever it is that you are feeling at the moment, let it be and then let it go. You have the power to choose. Choose freedom.

Past Imperfect, Choosing To Be Happy NOW

Today I was remembering a conversation I had with a man at a dinner party given by one of my friends some eleven years ago. I sat beside a man who was then in his early fifties, well groomed without being flashy, attractive and very funny. And I mean funny.

He started out by saying he was conceived stamped with a DNA code that says "not suitable for marriage", but he did get married anyway just to please his parents. He said he was the perfect family man for 12 years, had a little girl but then the code kicked in and he left the institution of marriage.

He loved his daughter and so when she said "Daddy, please buy a house close to this one so I can see you all the time" he did! For six years after the divorce he would come home to his ex-wife and daughter in the afternoons, go out at night, and then come home to his other home, close enough to his ex-wife and daughter's home, but private enough that he could have a live in girlfriend whose name and face changes quite often. It seems that he does not want to come home to an empty house, and if one relationship does not work out, there is always another one. He was lonely and he did not want to be lonely.

At the time of our conversation, the man who owned a company that manages 200 million dollars in stocks and other investments, from some Hollywood producers and few east coast trusts was a lonely man. He had lots of money but he was not happy. I have come to ask "What makes people happy". From my observation over the years, I have found that happy people have characteristics that set them apart from the rest.

The rest whom Henry David Thoreau calls "mass of men" who "lead lives of quiet desperation."

Beyond a certain level of comfort, when all of the physical needs are met: food, clothing, shelter, there is something different with happy people that it really does not matter whether they have millions of dollars in the bank or just having a career that they enjoy. It has very little to do with how much money they have.

I now know that these are the universal qualities of happy people.

1. Happy people have an inner strength. They do not need validation from others.

2. Happy people forgive the past wrongs that have been done them.
3. Happy people truly enjoy their work. They do their work because they can not imagine doing anything else.
4. Happy people choose their reactions to people and circumstances they encounter. They act rather than re-act.

Now let us discuss each and every one of these characteristics:

Happy people have an inner strength. They do not need validation from others.

Happy people do not need the constant approval of others for what they do or who they are. They are content with what they have become and constantly delight in the process of their evolution.

Happy people forgive the past wrongs that have been done them.

It would have been wonderful if all of us have perfect childhoods, but as I get older, I have come to realize that either all of us had it or none of us had it. It was what it was!

For each of us, whatever happened in the past was perfect for our stage in life. We are here now!

We can either go back to our childhood experiences and blame our parents, ourselves, anyone who had hurt us in the past and carry it with us for the rest of our lives or we can take responsibility for our feelings right here and right now.

We can choose to be imprisoned or walk free. The best part of it, is that WE can choose! Happy people have gone beyond their childhood pasts--imperfect as it seems-- and moved on.

They choose to forgive, forget and move on.

Happy people truly enjoy their work. They do their work because they can not imagine doing anything else. To these people, there is only a very fine line between work and play, and oftentimes, the distinction between the two disappear completely.

Happy people choose their reactions to events and to the people they encounter.

There is a beautiful passage in one of F. Scott Fitzgerald's short stories called "The Freshest Boy". In it is a sentence I will never forget:

"It is not given to us to know those rare moments when people are wide open, and the slightest touch can either wither or heal. A moment too late, and we can never reach them anymore in this world. They will not be cured by our most efficacious drugs or slain by our sharpest swords."

Everything in our lives, no matter how seemingly insignificant is a karmic event.

As long as we live we will encounter these events. We are all given the power to choose how we will react to them and to everyone around us. Our guide is our hearts. We realize the wholeness when we pay attention to what we choose to do in any event. Follow your heart and you will never go wrong.

All of the above qualifications can be summed up in one sentence, and you can choose to have it. And here it is:

Happy people are self-referring. Only the ones who can always go back to themselves and find strength deep within are capable of sustaining happiness regardless of the circumstance that surrounds them. They act rather than react, and they create rather than compete. To them, life itself is a gift to be enjoyed, and the rest of it? Icing.

Do you dare to be self referring? Do you dare to CHOOSE to be happy?

Questions That Have No Answers

This news article will always be etched in my memory. Several years ago, in Los Angeles, a couple of hoodlums hid from an opposing gang by entering a Buddhist monastery. The monks were sworn not to tell a lie but they were also sworn to protect anything that lives.

When the opposing gang came to the monastery, the two monks that were on duty refused to tell the opposing gang where the others were hiding. Subsequently the people who were trying to find the hiding opposing gang members beat the two monks because they would not speak.

Were the monks right or wrong?

There are questions posted to me by many people of which I have given answers that were only true to me.

I would very much like to know you would answer these questions yourself and if you have questions that you also find difficult to answer.

Q: Why did not the Buddha manifest world peace?
A: Why did Jesus Christ not take us all up when he ascended?

Q: I am in love with someone else. Should I leave my husband/wife/lover?
A: How do you feel about it?

Q: Why do people lie?
A: What is a lie?

Q: If there is a God and He/She/It is All powerful, why does He/She/It allow so much suffering in this world?
A: Peace is within you.

Q: I am in love with someone who belongs to another. What should I do?
A: There is nothing wrong with loving. You can love as much as you like. Just don't covet. The old maxim follows. If you can steal him or her from the person he or she is with...you know the rest.

Redefining Power

I must have listened to the beginning of Lord of the Rings I, The Fellowship of the Ring about a dozen times. I love Cate Blanchett's voice.

"It began with the forging of the great rings. Three were given to the elves, immortal, wisest and fairest of all beings, seven to the dwarf lords, great miners and craftsmen of the mountain ores, and nine..nine rings were gifted to the race of men, who above all else desire power. For within these rings was bound the strength and will to govern each race."

"What is power? In the jungle, power is used for survival. Man on the other hand desire power in order to have dominion over other men, be it via economic, social, political or personal means, or any combination thereof.

This is how we define worldly power. As such, empires were built. But empires also collapse and power is taken by the mightier in a battle.

If it is not taken away by an enemy, eventually, it fades in time, like everything else. Worldly power is temporary.

There is another kind of power: mystical power, which was handed to Moses (Exodus 4). According to some texts, advanced yogis can manifest extraordinary feats. Many examples are mentioned in Autobiography of a Yogi by Paramahansa Yogananda.

To the uninitiated, such manifestations appear magical. One who is so in tune with the unseen and unmeasured energies in this world can make things, seemingly impossible to happen, happen.
Few people in the world have not seen Harry Potter movies. We delight in the movies about magic because some part of us believes it is possible whether we admit it or not.

There are many ways to tap into mystical power. The path of the saints and the path of the yogis are paths to God, and along the way, power is acquired. To use such powers is an ultimate test.

It is said that some secret societies exist and that they teach you all the secrets of the universe. They promise you fame, fortune and practically anything you could want.

Sometimes when we embark on a spiritual journey and our minds have become quiet we stumble upon seemingly magical coincidences.

Sometimes we get curious and we get sidetracked. In our everyday lives, this power is manifested when our desires are fine tuned with faith and detachment. This is the combination of events that makes things happen instantaneously, as Deepak Chopra calls it, "instantaneous manifestation of desire."

Just remember the times when you have arrived at the supermarket and while the whole parking lot was full, a person happens to be just pulling out in time for you to park.

Coincidence? Perhaps. But what if it happens again and again?

You realize that you can, at will, influence events. You have tapped into your power, but eventually we realize that the whole power trip is a trap--a test.

I always go back to the pages in the Bible when Jesus came out of the forty day and night fasting and prayer, and He became hungry. The devil presented to Him the following offers:

Turn this stone into bread, jump off the pinnacle of this temple, and finally, worship me and I will give you dominion over the world for it has been handed to me.

The trap is so well presented, so simple. Just show me that you are the Son of God as you claim to be.

As I reflect on it over and over, I realized that Jesus could still be hungry because he was still in the flesh. That the devil uses quotations from the bible is most appealing to the human intellect, but the last one is more general and would appeal to a human far more than the first two.

All humans are tempted by power, presented in different packages.

I am brought back to the mythical king by Percy Bysshe Shelley, Ozymandias, when all that was left of a once mighty empire is a stone that reads "My name is Ozymandias, King of Kings. Look on My works, Ye mighty and despair."

All worldly power fades in time. It is the way things are. All we have to do is review the history of the once mighty empires.

Worldly power can be handed to us by birth as a karmic necessity, or we can acquire it by some means, and we can even enjoy it for a while, but eventually we will have to wake up from the illusion of this world.

"Love not the world, neither the things that are in the world. If any man love the world, the love of the Father is not in him."

Ultimately, only those who choose not to use power get to keep it, for with great power comes an even greater responsibility-the responsibility of choice-, as Anakin Skywalker had to face thus becoming Darth Vader, as modern day mystics have to face when people come to them asking for miracles and even as

Moses had to face after leading the Jews out of Egypt.

When I re- read the old testament when even Moses asked God to take his life when the people went back to their old ways after having been led out of bondage, I knew how much responsibility he had to carry.

We were born as humans only to have some time to play. It is borrowed time in a borrowed body. Our privilege is to be human, our responsibility is to always remember that we are on our way back to God.

It is the objective of our journey and we must not forget, no matter how fantastic the voyage may be.

When we have reached perfect communion with God, then all our worldly concerns vanish. We become rooted in the truth that all power belongs to God and we realize that this world is a dream which we can fashion to our desires but that eventually we have to wake up from this dream.

This awakening to our true nature and the realization of the mystical power in us all takes time and much effort. In involves going back on track consciously.

It involves the realization that we can not keep power unless we realize that the desire to have dominion over anything but our souls, is futile.

If we do not do it consciously, then we will experience pain as a means to remind us that we are disconnected from the source of all there is.

It is to me, the meaning of "Seek ye first the kingdom of God" for we are all beloved children of God.

Our ever present power is in the choices that we make, moment to moment, to remember who we are.

Remembering Who We Are

There is a Zen story I remember reading a long time ago so I cannot remember who to ascribe it to. I cannot remember if it was a tortoise or a frog, but in our story we will make it a tortoise.

Once a scorpion asked a tortoise to transport him across a body of water. The tortoise said: "But you are a scorpion, and you will bite me." The scorpion said, "Why would I do that? If I bite you we will both die!"

So the tortoise carried the scorpion across and while in the middle of the body of water, the scorpion did bite the tortoise and as they both began to sink, the tortoise asked the scorpion "Why did you do it? Now we will both die!"

The scorpion said. "It is my nature."

A female eagle chooses one mate in one lifetime but after laying two eggs, only one of which will survive, it spends it's time alone. It is a solitary bird. The mythical bird phoenix rises, does what it has to do burns itself to ashes and then rises again. When the lion roars, the whole jungle trembles. It is their nature.

I observe my dogs all the time. They are my constant companion while my teenage son goes and spends time with his friends. When they stretch, the whole body stretches.

When I do the dog pose in yoga, it requires absolute precision and conscious thought, yet it is very natural for the dogs.

The Tao and Zen disciplines emphasize naturalness, and yet this naturalness does not come easy for us human beings.

There is a world of difference between the way a Zen master serves tea properly and someone who has simply studied the art serving tea. The movements are the same. The difference is in their state of minds.

The only way to come to the real sense of naturalness as a human being is by the narrow path of discipline. There is no other way. To skip discipline will be to miss the whole point.

It is true that some of us do not need to go through as much training as the others because they have already done the work in previous lifetimes and in this lifetime there is only a quickening.
Most of us have to come from a space of ignorance that is only questioned in this

lifetime and therefore much work has to be done.

When we have gone through the narrow path of discipline then we can remember who we really are. And then every movement, every thought, every action is that of a human being. A spirit clothed in a body that is shed, lifetime after lifetime, fulfilling karmic necessities, sacred contracts.

We are each one of us eternal beings experiencing life on earth. Whole perfect, complete, luminous, nothing lacking. Separate yet parts of a whole. It is in this realization where all the paths to freedom converge. And then we can be natural. And perhaps we can even enjoy a cup of tea served by the Zen master in the same frame of mind.

Say Goodbye to Yesterday

I can remember taking my son back home when he was born. I had to leave him in the hospital for a few days to have his body temperature stabilize.

Oh I had such great expectations of motherhood. I bought all cotton diapers determined that I will be "eco friendly"...This lasted two days.

I was in the process of writing my dissertation. I thought, well, I have a computer at home, I only have a couple of more experiments to do, it will be a breeze.

It was bliss. I loved taking care of him. I almost always put my head on his heart when he slept. He slept so soundly. There was only one problem, he slept soundly for an hour or two and then he would wake up again.

Because of lack of sleep, my head was empty and there was nothing I could write about. I would read the sentences I wrote and would be incredulous that I even wrote it.

I had to make one of the hardest decisions in my life. To either take him home to the

Philippines for my family to take care of him while I finish my doctorate, or we can both go home together to the Philippines and have my family take care of both of us.

I chose the first one.

That was eighteen years ago. Today we were talking about a girl. How does he determine whether he wants her from the ego's standpoint or from the heart.

The answer was not easy.

If it is from the heart then he would be happy for the girl regardless of whether he is with him or not, as long as the girl is happy.

If it is from the ego, he would want to possess the girl and would be very unhappy if she chose someone else, and in this case, she had many other men to choose from.

Taking my son back to the Philippines was truly a yesterday, but even my going to the supermarket this afternoon to get his favorite dessert, is also a yesterday. It is done, in the past.

The NOW is when the past, present and future converge.

We can not undo the past. No one can. And yet for the majority of us, we hang on to it. The past hurts,the past victories.

We are almost always trapped by the memory of it.

If we could only see that NOW is when we have the power to create, to be fully in the NOW is the only objective of our life, and that our future is created in the NOW, we would always welcome the saying 'Say Goodbye to Yesterday' even if it happened only a few minutes back.

Seventeen Years of Zen or a Lifetime of Lessons

There, I said it. I have been doing sitting meditation for the last seventeen years. I still can not pluck flowers from thin air or make a room full of people dance or levitate. I know that these people exist.

I also know that they were trying to teach the others a lesson when they did these things that seemed to defy the natural laws, as we perceive it.

I was deeply influenced by the book written by Ram Dass called Journey of Awakening.

Indeed what fascinated me about him was that he seemed to be all I wanted to be when he decided to embark on his journey and leave everything and everyone behind.

I was touched by his courage and now I accept it as recognizing his path and walking it with complete abandon.

My journey began when I left home, for the first time, to attend graduate school. I had to cross continents. All of a sudden, I was by myself. There were times when I would be washing the dishes in the laboratory on Friday evenings and thinking "It is early and I could still catch the last bus to go home to my parents", and then I would realize that I actually have to buy the ticket and ride a plane and take a two hour drive from the airport to where they were, deep in the mountains of Quezon.

In high school, I wanted to be Ayn Rand. In college, I wanted to be Marie Curie. In graduate school, having been away from my parents for the first time, I felt lost, alone and unable to cope with the demands of a normal graduate student's life.

At least what I thought it should be. If my parents had not instilled in me a deep sense of faith as my anchor, I probably would have died of loneliness, or tried to kill myself.

The very same anchor that felt like a collar on my neck when I was growing up was what has allowed me to go on. And then I met my [now] former husband and I was happy again.

And in between then and now, there were so many events that happened enough to fill a book, but what does it really matter now?

Happy times are accentuated by sad times. The endless contrast in emotions give it fire and allow us to feel.

Our stories are all the same.

The names change, the highlights and the lows change, and yet, they are all the same. The human motives that we read about in the Bible and even in the Bhagavad Gita are all the same. It seemed so long ago, so far away and yet, sitting here thinking about all of the circumstances and events that lead me to where I am now, I am deeply, deeply grateful for everything.

Looking back, it looks like a movie that never ends. Even our spiritual trips. Our egos delight in all of these fascinating things.

 I did not experience any of the things that Ram Dass wrote in his books while I sat in meditation, but I have finally come to accept my life as a trip that never ends until I, we, go back to where we started.

Running in circles going nowhere. Yes, here I am. I never left.

Sunrise, Sunset, The Seasons of Our Lives and Arbitrary Values

Things are actually very simple. Solutions are simple. It is this simplicity that our minds refuse to accept that makes us blind to the simplicity. Somehow the mind thrives on the thrill of making things complicated. The complication entertains it.

Values are assigned. They are arbitrary and can change. It all depends on the frame of mind of the one perceiving the object, or anything in particular, the viewpoint of the perceiver. Note that it is the perceiver who creates the viewpoint.

In college, there was this engineering class which I enjoyed a lot. We were asked to look at an object and draw it to specifications from a vanishing viewpoint. It was fantastic because looking at the object from a certain perspective and multiple perspectives and to draw how it would look was a great exercise in imagination and precision.

The objective was to present object via a series of plates [drawings] that shows how the object would look, viewed it at different angles.

There is no limit to the number of plates one can submit, but there was a minimum for the grade.

I woke up the other day after connecting with my college classmates on Facebook, and realized, oh my.. we are now the adults and it is our children who are in college.

We are old in that sense, and for only a few moments that I was talking to one of them, I was brought back to the time I was eighteen years old and in college.

In that moment, I shifted my viewpoint from that of the mother of a college student, to the college student I was. It was fun!

 The vanishing viewpoint was instantaneous, but one thing was very clear. It was I who created the view points, took them away and formed another viewpoint.

What is the significance of this in business? One can look at any business decision with a very simplistic point of view. No need to agonize about anything.

I asked my son something like this the other day " In debate if the premise were wrong, what happens to the argument?"

He answered, "The argument presented is still valid based on the premise that was worked on." It made me smile, for a scientist who is open minded will always learn something from the experiment even if he proceeded to do the experiment with the wrong assumption, but only if he is open minded.

If the only thing one can get from a business decision that did not result in profit were to learn that you will or will not accept certain things for the sake of profit alone, it was well worth going through all the processes that led to the present moment.

The perceived "loss" has now been a gain. Strictly speaking, there are no such things as losses. We assign them and we can unassign them at will. This is true of any life decision, not only the ones that pertain to business.

The sun will always rise where we are on the surface of the earth we are occupying, so it will set. How long is arbitrary. In Alaska, there is 6 months of sun and six months of darkness, if my memory is correct.

I can look at my age as more than half a century had passed, or the beginning of the other half of the century. Frankly speaking, as I write this, I feel fantastic, so what does it really matter what one's age is?

How long must you hang on to the pain of the past? You can summon it at will if you want to experience pain. Or you can dismiss it to experience and move on.

Reassign your values and live a happier life.

Teacher Teach Thyself

I just spent thirty hours trying to put into a businessman's language what I had in mind for a business venture. I have done this dozens of times, for a different audience, and for a different purpose.

I had wanted to create a miracle drug that would totally wipe out cancer from the vocabulary of the future generation.

These days my aspirations are more modest.

I eagerly told someone dear to me about my progress and no sooner had I finished telling her all about my project than her habitual way of thinking comes up. There is too much money involved, it is too risky. Are you sure you want to do this? Are you sure?

I got angry. My first impulse was to lash. But I didn't. I just said I did my homework, as I always do, and found the project to be perfectly feasible and profitable in a year.

We have gone through the same conversations again and again and again. And then I got tired of going through the same thought process over and over again. I simply did not want to tell her what I was doing anymore. I just did them. And time and time again I gave her a chance to celebrate life with me!

I got angry because my ego wanted to be patted and be told "hey that is a wonderful idea! Let us brainstorm so we can do it together or I can help you iron the kinks". But it is too much to do that. Such a giant step to go out of our fear based thinking and habitual patterns of thought.

I know she means well. She has a good heart. She wants the best for me.

It is I who should address the chatter in my mind.

The Bodhisattvas Among Us

We look so far away to find our teachers, when they are right in front of us. I am convinced that our dogs and my son are Bodhisattvas come to teach me in this lifetime.

I am allergic to cats and I never wanted dogs since I found out that I am the one who would take care of them. Yet, I somehow felt that my son needed them.

The little one, Hershey, a russell terrier and a gift from one of my former students, is more like me many years ago. Intolerable. She still uses our living room as her bathroom even after a year. Day after day my patience is put to the test. The last one was too much. She visits the neighbors yard through holes under the hurricane fence and one day she brought home fleas! Blair, the black lab who has been with us for six years has never had fleas! It was a most trying time for me!

My son was bit a couple of times but I get bit every day! How can that be? The first time I found out she brought home fleas I told myself I would never forgive her for this torture! And then I realized the three of them own the house and I just live there.

What am I complaining about?

My son is a most unusual person in that he is able to bring me out of whatever mood I am in into a better place. He is somehow in tune with all of his surroundings and himself and he loves the dogs with such purity of heart he never even got upset when Hershey came home with fleas. Our black lab sleeps outside of my son's room.

Hershey sleeps on my son's computer chair. When he comes home in the afternoon, the two dogs are beside themselves with joy and the love is reciprocated! Everyday I see an example of pure love exchanged between the three of them. My teachers are right here. I live with them.

The Battlefield That is the Mind

There is no master more ruthless, no jungle more wild, and no fire more fierce and consuming than the reactive mind. Therefore the battlefield of the mind is the only one we have to conquer, the only prison we have to walk out of, and then we can realize we have always been free. Freedom is the true nature of our being.

The Chains that Bind Us

We are bound not only by material things but also by our emotional attachments. It is much easier to detach ourselves from things. Not so with people.

I ran away when I was 7 years old. Not away from my parents' home but to my parents home from my aunt and uncle's home 5 miles away from where my parents lived.

Even then I knew that it would be better if someone were with me so I took two of my friends from my uncle's neighborhood and we walked the five miles. We were young and it was fun. It took us two hours but time flew by.

I was lonely at my uncle's home. It was a summer vacation and my parents thought it would be nice for me to spend a week with my aunt and uncle who did not have children of their own. I was a living doll on loan for a week. After three days, I was homesick. I missed my mother but I missed my father most.

My mother was livid that I did what I did but my father just laughed and welcomed me in his arms, and within a couple of hours my aunt and uncle, frantic about not finding me, and the parents of my two friends came to our home, to get to take my friends home. I said goodbye knowing that it will be a long time before we get to see each other again. It was then that I knew what it was like to be attached.

One of my colleagues, a wise man, told me a very long time ago, that all relationships end, whether voluntarily or involuntarily.

At that time I thought, wow, that was not a very happy view of life, and yet it is the truth. Even if we love another during a lifetime, there is still death to contend with. Things are impermanent.

Ties are impermanent.

In the beginning of romantic love, two feelings are evidently felt: Fascination with the other person, a curiosity that is sustained for a period of time, and the promise of passion, sexual union. There is an illusion that the one person can sustain both with with one another.

I am thinking of the words fascination and passion. So vivid, so colorful, so intriguing.

Fascination comes every time there is something new and different.

Passion is a need to unite with the object of affection at the physical level.

Fascination ends and passion fades, in time. It is the nature of humans to get bored and tired of something no matter how good. It is only a matter of time.

Uncontrolled, passion can burn. While the object of passion is to unite with the object of affection it is without meaning unless both people have united at the level of the soul.

There is so much energy associated with passion that it is what is required to create. In some it is channeled to a great work of art. With the saints, the object of affection is God.

To use the energy of passion is the highest form of yoga. Tantra yoga.

It is not possible for anyone to sustain the fascination and passion of another, forever. To think so would be to delude oneself.

It follows that the only kind of relationship that would work long term is the one where there is no expectation beyond the bounds of common self respect. Treat the other person the way you want to be treated.

Moreover, you give what you desire the most not because of the hope for a return but because it is the most natural thing to do.

By this I mean that you do not disrespect the other because who you are really disrespecting yourself when you do so. By this I mean that honesty, trust, loyalty and understanding are implicit.

It is a relationship where either person is free to leave at any time and the other would be happy for the other person regardless.

In this case romantic love, the needy, clinging, grasping, possessing quality of it, is replaced by something entirely different. A soul connection. The kind that lets oneself and the other be. Like having your best friend. A mirror of yourself.

It is the kind of love that sees the other person just as he or she is, not through the illusion of perfection, but through the raw and naked quality of that person regardless of position in life, economic status and societal pressures.

I know that this kind of love exists. I saw it in my parents.

In this case the choice to be together is moment to moment rather than a promise of forever.

This is why I am afraid to be in love again. It is not because I am not able to love deeply, it is because I have not yet perfected this quality in my heart.

And when I have, I will know, and I will be free to love again. And I will offer it freely, without hope of return, without the need for a promise of forever, not even a wish for the person to acknowledge it.

For loving is it's own reward. It is a balm that heals both the giver and the receiver equally.

So I will love, unconditionally, freely and without bounds.

Eventually we will all have to give up all attachments to be really free. A free man does not single out another.

The distinction between love and hate, hope and fear, gain or loss, fame and shame must eventually be dissolved to have true freedom.

The kind of freedom that Buddha attained. I know I will have to do this sometime. We all do.

But for now I will love, live life and be happy.

For now, I will honor my karmic connections in this lifetime and hope that in so doing, I will still be on my path to true freedom.

The Cube as a Symbol of an Integrated Life

The cube is a symbol of stability. It is also a symbol of total balance. Sometimes it is used to symbolize truth. To me, the cube is a symbol of perfection, it is a symbol of an integrated life. An integrated life is a life led by an integrated person. In it, there is perfect harmony between wants and needs, be they spiritual, financial, physical, mental or relationship needs and wants. For each individual, such a perfect balance exists, and such balance can only be determined by the person living his or her life.

Paradoxically, achieving balance in all areas of our lives is not a static process but rather a very dynamic one. Our needs and wants change. Everything outside of us changes. Our bodies change. How then do we achieve this balance when everything changes? We must bring ourselves back to that which is immutable, our divine Self which is unchanging. It is pure, perfect, endowed with infinite wisdom and has within it all the knowledge required to make sound decisions. All we have to do is remember it.

When we remember this Self, we are in the moment, and all of our thoughts and actions or inactions are perfect for that moment. An integrated life is a series of perfect moments, arranged like pearls in a necklace that has no clasps.

The Eagle and the Phoenix

I have always been fascinated by eagles. I did not know much about them when I was little. There was no knowledge. The fascination originated from within, it was pure. An unquestionable connection every time I see their pictures.

I posted this state of mind at Twitter one and a half hour ago "The Diamond Sutra,the Sword of Manjushri, why eagles are solitary birds, and why the phoenix rises again and again. Mired in confusion, steeped in delusion."

And the answer came and the voice was very clear:

"The phoenix rises because it represents desire. The continual rise and destruction of desire in man. Now you figure out why the eagle is a solitary bird."

I laughed. The answer: "The eagle is a solitary bird because it has to fly very high and the other birds can not withstand the thinness of air at those altitudes. They will die. They travel alone because they have to go highest in order to see far, that they may report to the other eagles what they see. They can not afford the luxury of companionship because they neither want to take the burden of another or be a burden to another, as this will distract them from their true purpose, to see far ahead. In man it is the equivalent of the awakened mind, full of knowledge and endowed with wisdom. In order to get there, they have to travel alone and search the depths of their souls and risk perishing alone in that search."

And the Diamond Sutra which ends:

"Thus shall you think of this fleeting world:
A star at dawn, a bubble in a stream,
A flash of lightning in a summer cloud,
A flickering lamp, a phantom, and a dream"
alludes to the fate of the phoenix, and the Sword of Manjushri represents the discriminating awareness of the eagle and why it travels alone.

The Gap between Actuality and Reality, from the Unmanifest to Manifest and Our Shared Illusions

"We live in illusion and the appearance of things. There is a reality. We are that reality. When you understand this, you see that you are nothing, and being nothing, you are everything. That is all." ~ Kalu Rinpoche Journey of Awakening by Ram Dass

Today I was thinking of the movie "The Secret." It is one of the biggest hits in the history of publishing; surpassed only by the Harry Potter series...I could be wrong.

When it first came out, I bought a dozen of it and gave them to friends as present. In hindsight, I probably did them an injustice, because the manifestation process requires that one be so in tuned with this universe, but it really is not as simple as they portrayed in the movie.

There is a gap between thoughts and physical reality and that gap is not easily traversed. It is true that there are people who can manifest anything at will, but those very same people will not for they have to be responsible for the consequences of their creations.

The true manifestors create what they need and destroy at will. They have no need to hang on to anything or to own anything.

For this I will give an example where a devotee of Krishna, a King, who was at war with another kingdom. The King and his men had just finished a battle, lost heavily and needed to rest for the night to fight another battle in the morning. His men were tired and hungry as they had been fighting for a while. They came into an enchanted forest were there supposedly lived a hermit endowed with magical powers. When they got to the forest, the King removed his sandals and ordered his men to do the same, to show respect. Legend had it that this hermit was Krishna in human form.

After the King removed his sandals before entering the forest, the sage came out of nowhere and said, "O King, you have come to the right place. For tonight, you and your men shall rest and be entertained, for you have shown great respect by removing your sandals before going in and Lord Krishna is pleased. Please have your men unsaddle their horses and have the horses get food and water."

So the King and his men entered the forest and laid down their weapons and unsaddled their horses, and behold, a giant waterfalls appeared right before their very eyes, and a number of tents to shelter them for the night, and food, and wine, everything that a man could ever want for a feast. And beautiful women were serving his soldiers. And the horses were watered and fed, and the king was grateful to the hermit and to Lord Krishna.

When morning came, the men did not want to leave the forest to fight, they wanted to stay in the forest and be fed and pampered. But the King had a war to fight and so he went to the hermit and told him of his predicament. And the hermit blew a breath and the King and the men fell asleep and when they woke up, all the signs of what they experienced the night before were gone and the forest only had trees and a small stream, but they were rested and fed, and they saddled the horses to go and fight.

Was it just a dream? We can never tell. All men dreamt the same dream then. Very much like our universe.

Our universe is the manifestation of a collective consciousness. It cannot be undone. It can be rearranged much like the props in a stage play or an opera, but it is here. When those that can undo it decide, they have to have the collective agreement of those who built it in the first place. Unfortunately, some of those who agreed are no longer around and hence the seeming solidity of everything.

There is actuality and there is reality. We do not distinguish between the two, normally, but we must. The definitions in the Merriam Webster Online Dictionary are presented here.

Definition of ACTUALITY
1: the quality or state of being actual
2: something that is actual : fact, reality
— in actuality
: in actual fact
See actuality defined for English-language learners »

Examples of ACTUALITY
The actuality was quite different from the theory.

First Known Use of ACTUALITY
Related to ACTUALITY
Synonyms: existence, corporeality, corporeality, reality, subsistence, thingness
Antonyms: inexistence, nonbeing, nonexistence, nothingness, unreality
Definition of REALITY
1: the quality or state of being real
2a (1) : a real event, entity, or state of affairs (2) : the totality of real things and events
b : something that is neither derivative nor dependent but exists necessarily

3: television programming that features videos of actual occurrences (as a police chase, stunt, or natural disaster) —often used attributively
— in reality
: in actual fact
See reality defined for English-language learners »
Examples of REALITY
the difference between fiction and reality
The reality is that we can't afford to buy a house.
He used television as an escape from reality.
They made the plan a reality.
First Known Use of REALITY
Related to REALITY
Synonyms: actuality, case, materiality, fact
Antonyms: fantasy (also phantasy), fiction, illusion

We all live in illusion. The illusion of the solidity of things. A common agreement. When we create in thought, we have actuality. The physical world is a common reality and yet superimposed within it is another world that we can create and destroy at will, at any moment.

The best way I can think of to illustrate it at this point is that the phenomenal world is a stage. We are the crew. We can assume any role and we do, at any one point in time. We can rearrange the set, change the play, the characters, remove things, and add things to it. But we remain. We are the only constants.

When we realize this, the world ceases to be a battlefield, rather it becomes a garden to enjoy. Imagine being able to create a giant waterfalls at will. It does exist, if only in our minds, and in our minds, truly the world, or many worlds can be a playground. This is what the gift of the imagination is about.

The Geometry of Love

The most difficult lesson of all is Love. Why?

For this, I will ask you to take out a one dollar bill, in order to see the pyramid and "The Eye". Indeed the back of the one dollar bill is truly fascinating.

"The Eye" is represented in so many cultures to symbolize omnipresence it is hard to miss it.

For one second consider "The Eye" as Love and the bases of the pyramid as Truth, Beauty, Power and Wisdom, juxtaposed with each other and fully interchangeable, fully supporting each other.

Contrary to the popular saying, "Love is blind", Love sees fully what is behind the personalities and is able to go beyond the obvious. It is able to forgive and forget and start over.

On beauty, seen through the eyes of Love, everything is beautiful- for the one who loves truly relates to both the beauty and the grotesqueness of the person they love, in their wholeness and uniqueness.

With love comes Wisdom, the wisdom to endure momentary lapses when the ego tries to assert itself and demands something of the other person. For one who loves demands nothing and expects nothing knowing that in loving there is already an inherent gift. The capacity to love.

Power, oh, there is no power in the Universe greater than love. For God is love.

The Heart is a Lonely Hunter

There is a reason the heart features prominently in all spiritual paths. It holds the key to everything.

I am an auditory learner. I grew up on a farm in rural Philippines and we only had radios. There was no electricity. I can remember listening to "The Voice of America" and a show called "The Heart is a Lonely Hunter."

I was too young to relate to the romantic side of it, but I loved the music. I know it is by one of the classical composers but who it is escapes me right now.

The heart, truly is a lonely hunter. To hunt is not it's function. Its function is to give freely, without bounds and without expectations. Its function is to love unconditionally.

Unconditional love is the key to everything: every material desire, every relationship desire, literally, everything. To arrive at a space of unconditional love, one must work a lot on oneself.

To arrive at that space, where everything is possible and we can have every material desire fulfilled at will, we have to let go of all our egoistic identifications. We can pray, meditate, do yoga, the only object of which is to arrive at a perfect union with the Divine. There is no other way. Literally and figuratively it is the key to everything.

The heart is at the center of chakras whether coming up or down from the base to the seventh chakra. It is possible to open the third eye by using mantras. It is where all the psychic powers can be had, and yet, when the heart is not open then we are still on child's play, fulfilling egoistic needs with our psychic powers.

Nobody wants to block the heart consciously, and yet every time our egos get pricked and we respond to it , it is a heart blockage. We need to release everything.

In the past six weeks, I have been only "Listening to My Heart."

To get there I had to relate to the intense pain of looking within. While in deep meditations over many years, I experienced involuntary tears coming from my eyes a great number of times. I know this is a form of release for all of the pains I either dismissed or refused to acknowledge and all of my unconscious attachments. The tears no longer came after a certain point and I thought, wow, I have graduated from my attachments, finally! I was wrong!

I am a trained scientist and as such trained to only believe what I see, in the form of experiments. Even going through the process of looking within and recognizing where the pain was coming from, I had to look as an observer and look at the experiences with that training. Intense suffering is real, but it is intelligent. I can, at will, dismiss all of if by exhausting everything with the question "Why?" but that would be putting a band aid over a very deep gash, and in the long run it would not work. We ALL have to go to the roots of our suffering. It is the first Noble truth. Suffering springs from attachment. All attachments.

This time, when I cried during meditations, I KNEW why I was crying.

To relate to the ego we must work on ourselves via meditation or contemplation or prayer. Do what you think is best for you at the moment and then move on when it is necessary. We honor our paths.

Because I have been a student of spirituality for a long time, I can, at will, go into the Space of Unconditional Love with people I love. I call it a Sacred Space.

When I said at will it is because I choose to do so. Choosing is still ego's function. This is not what I am talking about. I am talking about being open hearted at times when it is difficult. The ego is so intelligent it can use everything to assert itself and lull us into THINKING we are free. The real test now comes from the heart. Are you able to trust your heart?

I do not recommend that you follow your instincts all the time. It is only at times when there is a conflict between logic and what your heart tells you that you follow your heart. Trust yourself. Trust your feelings.

I will always remember the scene from Star Wars when Luke Skywalker was trying to raise his spaceship from the marshes when he landed on Yoda's planet. He could do it at will for a few minutes and then it would sink again. The Yoda said "Trust your feelings, Luke"

To trust the heart? Completely? At first, no. Fear will be everywhere. Your ego will keep on saying "What are you doing? Why are you doing this? Are you crazy?" .Fear is the ego's way to project something in the future based on the past. A projection into the future from the memory of a past. Acknowledge that voice and give it a pat. Your ego is a friend, not an enemy.

How to get there? By the choices that we make, moment to moment, this is awareness. By contemplating on the heart while meditating, by praying for others, by forgiving, continuously, the perceived slights that we encounter day after day, and the most important, letting go of the past.

No matter how glorious or how sad it was, it is in the past. Let it go.

We only have NOW.

One other thing. If you choose the path of prayer, it is true, "Ask and It is Given." Behind that is the proviso, ask for absolute surrender [which gets rid of the ego based desires] perfect faith [which gives you detachment] and a pure heart [which only knows unconditional love and therefore you will only get what is good for you]

The Lesson of the Kobayashi Maru

I love the old Star Trek series. I watched whatever episode was on, no matter if I had seen it five times earlier. It is a testament to the superb talent of Gene Rodenberry.

The Kobayashi Maru was a game designed to test the reaction of a soldier, a warrior, an officer and a man or woman faced with unbeatable odds. Kirk reprogrammed it,. Technically, it is cheating.

I see it from a whole different perspective. It is man's will to survive. It is inherent in him. When Kirk reprogrammed the computer so that he can beat the game..and he was the only one at the Starfleet Academy who did so, he merely practiced ingenuity.

Spock got what he wanted. The reaction of a human being. Probably not what he would have liked but a reaction nevertheless.

I must admit that growing up I identified more with Spock than I did with Kirk. I am fascinated by logic, but sooner or later I realized that logic has limits.

In much the same way the writings of Ayn Rand mesmerized me from the time I was 12 years old, over a span of many, many years, and then I also realized the limits of such an ideal.

It does not account for the gamut of human emotions that make us all alive, the fires of passion that makes us all, humans.

And this is the same reason I go back to my old KJV again and again ..tattered from so many years of use and read about David the King, again and again.

He was, just like us, human.

The Origin of Desire

Most of the artwork that I was exposed to and still remember were from a class I took in college where we had to analyze paintings after paintings. In my English classes, we analyzed and wrote about books after books.

To interpret creative expressions is merely to learn about the artist, to take a tiny glimpse of his mind. We can never really write about the hows and whys.

Classical music I have loved since I was little, not knowing who the composers were or what the titles were until much later. I enjoyed it then as I do now. There was no need to interpret.

The mind is to me the most fascinating attribute of human beings. From it came Van Gogh's paintings, Mozart's concertos, Rodin's sculptures, Da Vinci's contributions in many fields, and the magnificent films that I am so very fond of. Yes, I consider films as a great artform, as I do prose and poetry.

Great minds with a desire for expression. The mind can be a tool for creation as well as a means to device destruction.

The television in my home is approaching 34 years, as are the stove and the refrigerator. They all work fine, and maybe someday I will have to buy new ones but for now, they are perfect for my needs. We do not subscribe to cable television for the very reason that I really like to watch television.

In my friend's home is a very big screen television and I am allowed to flip the channels as much as I like when I visit. There appears to be 200 some channels that are available to watch. One channel that I stayed longer had the royal tots..sons and daughters of the rich and famous and their toys. The show flashed miniature Jaguars and Ferraris and real ponies as their toys as well as lavish parties for the birthdays.

That was interesting, but what was more interesting was that presently, the Sultan of Brunei has a royal palace that can fit several White Houses!

A few years back, the Sultan of Brunei was the richest man in the world. Reportedly he had $40 billion dollars. At that time, Bill Gates reportedly had $6.7 billion. Things change as everything does.

Desire is a very basic human emotion, whether it be a desire for power or for recognition or for wealth. The question remains. Why? Every thought, every action has a karmic origin. Each and everyone of us is here to fulfill a unique purpose. It is up to us to find out what that purpose is and then perhaps we will understand our situations in life much better.

The Sultan of Brunei, the other billionaires and the homeless, as we all did, chose to be born in this lifetime to fulfill a role. We chose that role a long time back. The heads of States, those endowed with great wealth and power have great privileges and with it comes great responsibility. Consider though that there is something that equalizes all of us. The breath of life, the great equalizer.

The Pain of Cutting Out Frivolities

I remember having to spank my only child one day when he was very little. I was crying on the inside while I was doing it but it needed to be done. It was for his own good.

I had to write a quite painful letter the other day. It was to cut off communications with someone I was, and still am, quite fond of. A beloved friend. I did not want to do it but it was necessary.

I had to examine why it was painful. It was because I had to confront my own emotions, the ones that I consider improper and not worthy of me. Not only am I vain, I am also spiritually materialistic. The paradox is that as one becomes spiritually materialistic, it is the same time that one becomes spiritually bankrupt.

There are feelings that we categorize as "not belonging" to a spiritually mature individual: jealousy, rage, envy, thoughts of vengeance, possessiveness. These are considered "bad" feelings.

To develop fearlessness is to confront that which we fear face to face.

This is what is painful. When one decides that it is time to sever one's relationship to rejecting these feelings as bad, a radical severance is required. It is painful to cut through frivolity because we want to hang on to it. It is our nature to want to do so.

Frivolity comes in many forms, not necessarily as simple as vanity paying so much attention to how one looks physically. It could take the form of greed in the sense of spiritual progress. This is even more dangerous than simple vanity.

Just like an umbilical cord that needs to be cut, one has to have a ruthless compassion towards oneself when using the Sword of Manjusri. Above all else, it requires absolute honesty with oneself, to accept rather than shove under the rug, to be able to say yes they are there, these feelings and that they do not necessarily diminish oneself.

These feelings are thoughts, fueled with emotions, but when we relate to them fully we find that just like everything else, they pass. To reject them is to empower them and to empower them is to not recognize the fact that like everything else, they are an avenue to freedom.

On the one hand, while it is painful to acknowledge these emotions, facing them with the Sword of Manjusri allows one to do the right thing for oneself- to realize that to progress on the path to freedom, one has to cut through frivolities, not of one's relationship with others but with oneself, and to transmute the fiery nature of emotions.

To become fearless is to reclaim authentic power and to know that everything, every event, every person that we meet, we created in order to usher us to absolute freedom. We invited them there at the deepest level because in the more encompassing view, our objective is to realize that only our thoughts separate us from others.

So we acknowledge that the other person or event was not the cause of anger, it is rather oneself rejecting feelings as they come and questioning why they arise when one is supposed to be above them. We accept that we have them, we do not hang on to them, we do not act on them, rather we observe them. This is discriminating awareness.

And we give thanks for all that there was and hope that in some way we have enriched someone else's life if only for a short time, and that to let them grow, we have to respect their free wills and honor their paths.

*Manjusri is the god of discriminating awareness. In the Buddhist literature, his flaming sword is the symbol of wisdom and ruthless compassion, the one that cuts through all duality, arrogance and frivolity.

The Power of Decision : Allowing Inner Conflict

One of my business clients wanted a modest estate for a new home. He had found so many to look at but his heart was set on this one. He wanted it. It was his hearts' desire.

To my amazement and pure delight, he created a situation where the unusual became possible. When on the verge of getting it, he decided he did not want it after all.

This is a real life situation. The fascinating thing about it from my point of view is the ability of one man to desire something so much that his desire fueled a series of events that would lead to what he THOUGHT he wanted.

It reminds me of the episode where Spock's future wife created a situation where she would end up the victor regardless of what happens, and Spock telling her in the end that "You will find that having is not the same as wanting."

The Price of Fundamental Freedom

There is a price for finding fundamental freedom. Aloneness.

Chogyam Trungpa describes it perfectly.

"It is like living among snow capped peaks with clouds wrapped around them and the sun and the moon shining brightly. Below tall trees are swayed by the howling winds and beneath them is a thundering waterfall.

From our point of view, we may appreciate this desolation if we are an occasional tourist who photographs it or a mountain climber trying to climb the mountain top but we do not really want to live in those places. It's no fun. It is terrifying, terrible." ~ Chogyam Trungpa in "The Myth of Freedom and the Way of Meditation

This is what Jesus Christ meant when he said "Where I am going I you can not follow but later you will follow". John 13:36 KJV

It is what St. John of the Cross wrote about: The dark night of the soul.

In that place, there is no one to catch you if you fall.

You are all alone and you have to deal with it. There is a natural tendency to want to take others with you. The ego wants this because it is another way of validating yourself.

You want to go back, escape, but there is no escape.

The stages of awakening follows if at first you don't go insane.

First, dealing with boredom, relating with the neurosis of your mind and befriending your ego instead of fighting it.

The way of the Bodhisattva and then the way of the warrior.

Then upon surrendering, seeing the universe dance at your feet, bliss.

One can, and some do, stay in this stage for eons. Sooner or later, one has to deal with aloneness, the inevitable aloneness that comes after the bliss.

This is when one decides to step in to the gateway of the unknown or go back to the way it was and start all over. Another lifetime.

And then, perhaps, one day one can come back and show others The Path. Coming down from the snow peaked mountains is much faster, for now the clouds have parted and the sun illuminates everything and for the first time one sees that it was impossible to fall. One had to experience the fear. It was part of the test.

The Quicksands of Our Thoughts

We all like the familiar. There is comfort in it. We know the terrain no matter how full of prickly shrubbery. We don't mind the wounds that we gather as we tread along because we are used to it.

We see another path yonder but it leads to the unknown and the unknown is always scary, so we keep ignoring the wounds that we gather as we continue on our familiar paths or we stand still and get fascinated by the scars that we have gathered. The quicksands of our thoughts.

I have observed my own thoughts as I interact with others. My own suffering is brought about by an intense desire to fix things for others, to make people do things that I think will make them whole again.

It is an illusion that they are broken.

They have always been on the right path because it is their choice to be so. I am the one caught up in the quicksand of my thoughts and when I have stopped resisting the present moment, perhaps there is a way out.

Perhaps there is a way out, in this lifetime or the next.

The Two Faces of Janus

Why would a god have two faces one facing the opposite direction from the other, I wonder.

Janus is the Roman god which symbolized gateways,endings and new beginnings. The first month of the year which symbolizes new beginnings, January, was named after Janus. Where the two faces meet, the future and the past is the NOW. It is what we always overlook as we are conditioned to either hang on to the past or pine for the future.

If we assume that the two faces each has a 180 latitude line of sight the two line of visions can never meet. Parallel lines never meet and in Janus the distance between the two parallel lines, the gap is the NOW.

When we are fully in the NOW, we do not regret the past nor worry about the future. We know they exist, but in reality they are all relative to the NOW. We realize that in this gap the nature of all phenomena lies, and that where there is a seeming duality, there is in fact unity.

In the question lies part of the answer. Where does the other part come from? From within.

An honest coin has two sides. When we accept this seeming duality as an illusion we are entering into the NOW.

The Value of Impermanence

I love old things. They have character. They are embedded with the essence of the previous owners.

The ruins of the great empires remind us that things, everything is impermanent.

Relationships end, material things decay, contributions of the great minds fade away and are forgotten, unless someone brings it back and revive.

Nothing lasts forever. Impermanence is the nature of all phenomena which brings us to where we are.

Thoughts, feelings, things, do not last and we can either look at it with joy or with sadness or we can enjoy the moment when we have it. Whether we like it or not, our children will grow old.

Whether we like it or not, we have a finite use of the body we are in.

One can use the sword of discrimination to cut off the tendency of the mind to consistently distinguish between this and that. On the one hand, we can enjoy where we are and what we have in the moment, right at this moment and know that the memories that we create in this moment can be summoned at will, on the other hand, we have to prepare to let things, people and relationships go. When we are able to reconcile the two then we know that each moment is as perfect as it should be. Nothing lacking.

And the next moment is new, as fresh as the sun rising from the horizon, or the smell of the earth after it has just rained, or the cool crisp morning air, or very simply looking at the world through a child's eyes, again and again.

It is in these moments when the perceived failures of the past are erased and replaced with the infinite possibilities of the present.

To Covet

This definition was from the Merriam-Webster dictionary online

Main Entry: cov·et
Pronunciation: \'k?-v?t\

Function: verb
Etymology: Middle English coveiten, from Anglo-French coveiter, from Vulgar Latin*cupidietare,from Latin cupiditat-, cupiditas desire, from cupidus desirous, from cupere to desire

Date: 14th century
transitive verb1 : to wish for earnestly <covet an award>
2 : to desire (what belongs to another) inordinately or culpablyintransitive verb: to feel inordinate desire for what belongs to another
synonyms see desire
— cov·et·able \-v?-t?-b?l\ adjective
— cov·et·er \-t?r\ noun
— cov·et·ing·ly \-ti?-le\ adverb

Why do we covet? The earliest example of covetousness I have been exposed to is with

Abel and Cain, in the Bible. And then there was King David who coveted Bathsheba.

One of the possible answers is because we were programmed into it. I will not go into the details of this. I can only give you the examples from experience as I had them.

As a child I knew the fine things in life. There was something different, a memory of some distant past so my preferences have always been different. I knew what real lace was, what a goblet was, what heavenly music from the classical masters were even before I knew their names.

This is entirely out of context into the setting I was born to. I grew up on a farm but having had comfortable relatives on my mother's side of the family allowed me to witness and be part of a different side of life. Affluence in the city in stark contrast to the simple life on a farm. Somehow I felt at ease on both settings, without much effort.

As a child,there were times that I did covet those fine things that my cousins had. It felt bad. Luckily, I was very fortunate that there were no people that I loved the most other than my parents and I listened to them when I was a child. Not out of fear but out of deep love. I learned much, and early on.

I know what it is to want something so badly my thoughts could almost be carved in stone. I have experienced it in all areas of my life: love, family, career, the outside world.

We all buy into this one way or another one time or another and every once in a while, it will pop up. We are bombarded with these messages every day of our lives. The message is "To be rich and famous is to be happy therefore pursue everything that will make you rich and famous, then you will be happy."

In my case, I simply wanted to win the Nobel Prize in Chemistry or Medicine and Physiology. So my carrot was fame, in Science.

Most of us would like to be wealthy. I never dismissed it, but it was not what motivated me.

The sages have long known that this world is no more than an illusion, but it is so real to us. As he meditates, he sits like a rock, untouched by the whirling of the winds of the mind and knows that the whole world is contained within him. What is there to covet?

I will insert here a story that makes me laugh each and every time. For the record, it took me ten years of work to appreciate the humour in this story, or for that matter to solve one koan.

I was simply living life as I knew it, bound by the shackles of my own mind.

So the story goes:

A scholar went to see a renowned sage. He was in competition with one other scholar and wishes to beat him as to which one would have the better, deeper knowledge.

They each went their separate ways and decided to meet after a certain time.

But the sage knew what he was up to so he kept mostly silent while the scholar was learning from him, writing every word that the sage uttered and analyzing them. All this time, this scholar who was scion to a Brahmin family served as a servant to the sage.

His desire to beat his competition was fierce.

As the sage was aware of his motives, he now told the scholar that when he comes back he would have to pay for the teaching, in gold.

After a few years...yes, a few years, when the time to meet his competitor came he was armed with volumes and volumes of journal. The competitor thought he was beaten, so on their way back to the University, he managed to get rid of the volumes of material that the scholar wrote.

The scholar cried in anguish and decided he will go back to the sage.

He worked for a few years to save enough money to pay the sage. When he came back to the sage, he gave him only part of his savings in the form of gold dust so that he could still have some money left.

But the sage demanded more and more or he would not begin the teaching. The scholar was furious and frustrated at the same time but he wanted the teaching so much, he gave the sage the whole pouch.

When the sage knew that there was nothing left from the scholar, he could not even pay for his way home, the sage danced in joy while throwing away the gold dust in the river.

The scholar almost went insane. Almost. The sage then turned to him and said "You fool. What do I need the gold dust for? The whole world is gold to me.

Do you really think you can buy my teachings for a pouch filled with gold? You will now have to serve me for ten years as a servant for me to teach you anything."

Needless to say, those ten years tested everything that the scholar was hanging on to. It became thirty years later before he went back to his hometown. At any time, he was free to leave the sage and go back, he was told. He would be provided for transport and food.

And he did find what he was looking for.

To rediscover what we have forgotten is a lifetime quest. Sometimes it will involve many lifetimes. We have to look into our minds but not while we are in it! Otherwise we will be like the worm that makes silk. We spin and spin and spin silk until we are so enclosed in it that we suffocate.

This is what meditation/prayer/contemplation teaches us, to be able to see that we are willing prisoners of our minds.

Unfortunately there is no one who can do this for us. We have to do it on our own in our own time. There are no right or wrong decisions per se. There are only pathways, if we care to look.

Covetousness is a result of fundamental belief in lack. This is what we debunk when we go into meditation.

I end this with the normal disclaimer. There is nothing wrong with desire or with being rich and famous if that is your passion . Desire in and by itself is how we manifest things into this physical reality.

You honor it until the time when you are ready to look for something else. You honor yourself and your path. But every once in a while, ask yourself : Are these really your goals or are they programmed into you?

"You are what your deep driving desire is. As your deep driving desire, so is your will, as your will so is your deed, as your deed, so is your destiny"-The Upanishads.

What is your deep driving desire?

True Freedom is of the Spirit

I was just telling a couple of my friends today that it seems I am almost always running away. But from what I do not know. And then I remembered my mother. She was exacting, demanding, unyielding, uncompromising, and most of all, unbound. She had true freedom of the spirit. And that was probably why when I was growing up, I did not like her that much. She was different from the mothers of the other children. And now, I realize,I have become her except for one thing. She was a free spirit from the time she was a child. I am not, even now.

Oh, but there is a chasm of difference between our childhoods. My mother was the first born to a land baron who granted her every wish. I was born the fifth girl to a man from a fisherman's family. When they met, my father's only possessions were wisdom and love. Even then she did not care much about material things. I cannot say the same about me when I was her age. My mother loved and married my father with absolute certainty that even when I had never seen them display affection for each other in public,I could never remember them raising voices to each other.

My mother exchanged medical school for a family with my father. As a child, thinking like an adult in that society, I never would have approved of that marriage, so I understood my maternal grandparents somewhat. Still, understanding is different from compassion. The first one, intellectual, the other comes from the heart. One is immediate, the other takes years of self inquiry to develop.

My mother was so fiercely independent that even after her stroke and after having to relearn the simple things such as holding a cup of tea, and trying to write again, during the years while she was undergoing physical therapy, she refused to be served by me! I thought it was stubborn and stupid since I could do things a lot faster than she could but it was an assertion of the human spirit.

Freedom is of the spirit. It has little to do with the circumstances outside of ourselves. An example of this would be that of Alexandr Solzhenitsyn who, imprisoned in Siberia, wrote Gulag Archipelago and won the Nobel Peace Prize.

We take our liberties for granted until it is taken away from us, and yet even with outwardly free surroundings, one can still feel trapped. It is the spirit that needs to be freed. The body, the personality is only a vessel.

With so many years of education, travel, training, meeting people from all over, going through what people tell me would take them a long time to have done, I am at heart still the child who had only been secure in the presence of my father. The one person who treated me like the son that he wanted so much and loved me unconditionally, without trying to understand. No matter that I was born a girl.

Perhaps, in this lifetime I can even hope to be free and not be afraid to find out who I am. Who is this behind the personality that has lucid dreams of the past? Why do I dream such dreams? Why am I always running away?

Why is it that I relate to Spock a lot more than I do James T. Kirk in the old Star Trek? And just like Spock, I am secretly amused by the humanity of Captain Kirk, and yet I admire it so. Ok. I was just kidding. Or am I?

True Surrender Results in Peace

I should have titled this piece "And the Joke Was on Me" for many reasons. Firstly, I realized that I was what Chogyam Trungpa described as rigidly solid. I have been doing sitting meditation for so many years, "disciplining" myself. It is all so hilarious now.

On Saturdays I usually do ten hours of meditation. No matter what happens. Sometimes the body gives way after 8 hours and I stop.

Yesterday I had so many demands on my time and I chose to attend to them instead of doing my sitting. My mind was agitated and I kept questioning why now? After all, I have done so many hours of sitting. My peace of mind was disturbed because of an unusual dream. But I was thinking, how can this be? I was so peaceful all week! Here I was following all the rules of surrendering to the heart, and yet my peace was feeble, not imperturbable at all! How can a dream, a creation of my ego do this?

After two hours of sitting, instead of doing eight more hours of sitting, I went out for a walk and I looked at the moon and it was peaceful and calm and it was cool and all of a sudden I realized this is all an illusion, a dream within a dream within a dream and I can dismiss all of it, at will. Even the cause of my agitation.

When I came back, I pulled out my copy of Chogyam Trungpa's "The Myth of Freedom" and started reading for at least the 100th time. And then I started laughing and laughing and laughing at myself.

I realized how seriously I had been taking life. So rigid, so disciplined, so closed! No room for learning. I fancied myself liberated but what I had done instead was reinforced my ego! Oh...that was so funny.

"I started a joke and the joke was on me" as the song goes.

Our True Legacy to Our Children

My son and I are very fortunate to live in a small town with all the amenities of the big city and the feel and flavor of the country.

By this I mean that my son's classmates, with few exceptions, live within 2 miles of our home.

He has known his friends since elementary school and they have grown up together. Their mothers and I have shared birthday parties at the paintball places, skating rinks, rollerblading places, parks,and each other's homes. We have exchanged sleep overs over the years.

One of the most important characteristics of Lafayette, Louisiana is that all the parents that I know are involved with everything their children are involved with. During soccer season, we conglomerated on soccer parks for tournaments. It is an ideal place to raise a balanced child.

Whether we like it or not, our children become teenagers. There are so many things that they get absorbed in.

Our task is to balance involvement with some degree of freedom. In Zen practice, it is called the middle way. Not too heavy and not too light. The middle way.

As a parent, it was hardest for me to give my son the freedom other parents allow, but I have to have faith that my child would do the right thing when confronted with difficult choices.

I was born and raised in an entirely different culture where our hierarchy was God, parents, teachers. We viewed our parents as extensions of God and therefore, omniscient and infallible.

Next to our parents, we revered our teachers.

But this is America and the challenges are different, even if the principles are the same.

We simply accept our children as ordinary human beings, just like us. Everything that we need, they need.

This means unconditional acceptance and unbounded love. By unbounded love, I do not mean foolish love. Children will always push the limits of our patience in order to know their boundaries, but setting the boundaries is as simple as telling the truth as it is.

It is as simple as saying "Your curfew is at this time and when you are not home, I worry about whether you had a flat tire and could not reach me or you got stranded somewhere, so please come home on time." There.

Children have an immense capacity to understand us. We simply recognize that. Mostly, what they want is attention and affection, just like we do.

One of the best things I love about my son is that when I talk to him, about anything, he actually removes the headset from his ears, turns his swivel chair around so that the computer is behind him, and looks into my eyes when I am speaking.

He pays full attention even for just a few minutes. On the other hand, I am also prepared to hear, "I cannot talk right now." We can give them the same, no matter what we are doing.

Simple courtesy is another thing we give our children. We never enter their rooms unannounced, leaving things the way they are in their rooms when we do go there. They have a right to privacy as much as we do.

Where Heaven and Earth Meet, the Heart

Meditation on the Heart as Your Center for Manifesting

The heart is the energy center where all manifestation begins. This is why we say I wish with all my heart that...

It is possible to begin manifestation directly from the heart, to not deal with energies, if and only if one has already done the discipline of meditation or deep contemplation as in the case of saints. For everyone else who are just beginning, the following exercise is recommended to remove blockages in the body's energy conduit.

Before one begins, I must caution that this exercise has little to do with the Vehicle of direct energy, Tantra. For that both the Hinayana and the Mahayana vehicles must have been mastered. I am afraid there are no shortcuts. [For further reading, use Chogyam Trungpa's books, Meditation in Action, Cutting Through Spiritual Materialism and Shambhala, the Sacred Path of the Warrior]

We will simply call this exercise as clearing the path.

This exercise may propel you to activate kundalini and unless both the body and the mind are sufficiently purified, you may not be able to handle the surge of energy through your body. The most important part is to pay attention to the reaction of your body and then document it after the exercise. You may do this exercise standing up or sitting in half lotus or full lotus position.

Imagine yourself at the center of an hour-glass. Now imagine that your heart is at the center of that hour glass. This hour glass is unusual because the top is one half circle and the bottom is the other half circle. The top looks like a wine glass with very short stem and is connected to the other half with that stem. That stem is where your heart is.

Now envision a flexible tube or cord that runs from the base of our spine to the center of the earth and you are now connected to the core of the earth. The base of your spine is the first Chakra. It is the color of the finest ruby. Red, not blood red but dark red and brilliant. This ruby red ball is floating right inside your spine and you can see it as pure as the finest ruby. No imperfections. Breathe through your first chakra and feel the energy coming from the center of the earth to your first chakra.

Follow the energy going from the first chakra to the second chakra which is 3 inches above the base of your spine. There is an orange ball there brilliant and pure, like an orange except that is luminous. Breathe three times into the brilliant orange ball.

Follow the energy to the area of the solar plexus, three inches below the navel. Breathe into it. This is the third chakra and its color is yellow, like the sun. Again you imagine that this yellow ball is floating inside the body not held by anything. Breathe into it three times.

Follow the energy from the third chakra into your heart center. The color of the ball is luminous green. Stay there. Breathe into it and through it. You can expand the green ball as much as you like. Feel it. Feel your heart center opening. Breathing in love, breathing out love. How does it feel?

Relax and get centered.

Now imagine that the energy is now going from your heart center into your throat area and that in that throat area is a blue ball just floating. The fifth chakra has the color blue like the deep blue ocean. Breathe into it three times. Follow the energy from the throat into the sixth chakra, which is your third eye. Again breathe into it and imagine that it opens little by little as you breathe into it. Like a baby's eyes the first time he wakes up in the morning.

Now imagine the energy flowing up from your sixth chakra into the crown of your head. Above the physical skull, a violet ball that symbolizes the awakened mind. Breathe into this ball three times. Pause.

Splitting the energy beam.

Imagine a beam of light coming from space. You see no beginning or end to this. The beam of light is like a laser beam of pure white light focused on the crown chakra. As it enters the crown chakra follow the flow of this light through all the centers as you breathe through all the centers, stopping at the root chakra.

When your attention is at the root chakra, imagine that the cord connecting you to the center of the earth is now connected to this energy flow which started from the crown of your head. There is now free exchange and continuous flow of energy up and down. A dance. Your body has become a conduit of energy.

The last step is continuing the flow of energy from both ends, from both the root chakra connected to the center of the earth and from the crown chakra. This time the energy going into the crown chakra is used to create a spiral that envelopes your body and then the energy spiral which begun in the crown chakra now ends at the root chakra, merging with the energy from the cord and now simply going up the other centers.

Write the feeling after you do this meditation and keep a journal for all the times you meditate using this method.

When Every Event Becomes a Gateway

As I write this I am laughing at myself. Several years ago I would have considered what I did today absolutely insane. Perhaps it still is. Who knows? It is hilarious at any angle.

Yesterday I told one of my contacts on Facebook that I did not like his picture and would he please change it? How rude! The fact is that he is a very handsome man and I loved the picture of him and his wife together but I did not like the picture where he was alone. It reminded me of someone. What happened was a series of emails where he refused to change his picture and I ended up telling him and his wife my life story. Aha!

In remembering an old friend and trying to erase his memory by asking someone to change their picture on my contacts list, I found two friends, him and his wife. What was remarkable was that this man understood me! And he reminded me what of what I have been trying to teach everyone. Forget the past, live in the NOW. The present is much more exciting, full of promises, full of hope.

He told me that he too did past life regressions and only uses them in the context of the present moment.

We never know when and where we will get our next lesson.

Vast like the Ocean, Endless like the Sky

The space in between thoughts, where the primordial sound of "Aum" reverberates is vast like the ocean, endless like the sky.

There was one night a while back when I entered into a state of delta. I was neither asleep nor awake. My eyes were closed and my body was still but my mind was somewhere else. I was in the gap between thoughts and aware of it.

When I was little, out of body experience was common place for me. I did not want it. It scared me to see myself pass through walls and high above the trees into the vast space, while looking at my sleeping physical body below.

My higher Self obeyed. I was not ready for it. Now, I am not able to do it at will.

Perhaps in the future when my thoughts and feelings are as pure as when I was a child, I can, and will do it again. The many years of education allowed me to dismiss it all as delusion. I now know it never was.

Nevertheless, I have no burning desire to do it at will.

On this particular weekend night when I had done sequential meditation, I fell asleep. I was troubled with emotional questions. I was in emotional pain. To alleviate the pain I forced myself to sit longer.

I have had no trouble falling asleep under any circumstances. Once my back hit the bed, I was out.

I could see myself lying on the bed covered with my comforter and yet I was in a dome of light, beautiful dancing lights, luminous, variegated, as if a thousand rainbows merged, that changes colors as my friend and I danced. Our spirits danced.

We were just like children playing. There was nothing sexual about it. It was pure delight. It was a dome of unconditional love. A space where every material desire can be had at will, and yet, I wished for nothing else other than that moment. It is what pure love is. Nothing to give, nothing to receive, nothing to want.

We stayed there for a long time. I looked at the clock when I got up. According to earth time, it was four hours,yet it seemed so short! Time did not exist there.

I awoke and felt like I was asleep for a whole day.

When an Action is Complete

This story has been mentioned in many Zen books.

Two monks, one who was just starting his study and one who has been a monk for a long time were on a trip to study with another Zen master. While traveling came upon a woman who wanted to cross the river but did not want her clothes to get wet. As purity of mind and body was an important lesson, the old monk refused. The young monk on the other hand merrily carried the woman on his shoulders across the river, and afterwards, they went on their way and she went her way.

A long time has passed and the old monk finally spoke, reprimanding the young monk. "I can not believe you carried her across the river. We were not supposed to have bodily contact with a woman!", the old monk said to the young one in a self-righteous tone. The young monk answered "Friend, I carried her across the river several hours ago and then I put her down. You are still carrying her on your shoulders."

When I look around my house and see clutter, I am reminded of my friend who owns a house that is four times as big. She keeps it almost always, immaculate. She hires no one to clean it for her. Very simply, she puts everything away as she is done with them. When she cooks, as soon as the meal preparation is complete, the kitchen would be spotless, as if no activity had occurred there and the sumptuous meal just magically appeared on the table. She does all actions completely, no traces left. This is how she does everything in her daily life, always, completely in the moment.

Our minds are so filled with desires, unfinished projects, reminders of what to do tomorrow and plans for the future we tend to do multitasking. It is not possible to do two things simultaneously and be fully present. We delude ourselves into thinking that we can but if we simply look inward honestly, we will see that what we have is unfinished tasks, unfinished business.

To cultivate moment to moment awareness, to finish something completely, requires one pointed focus on the task at hand. It is as if we were burning a log and when it is done, only the ashes are left. It is true whether we are folding clothes or washing the dishes or negotiating a complicated business deal We do not look back and judge.

The next moment is a new moment. Another task begins and we see the completion of it. When we can cultivate this, we see space. Once in a while, we get a glimpse of freedom.

The Price of Fundamental Freedom

There is a price for finding fundamental freedom. Aloneness.

Chogyam Trungpa describes it perfectly.

"It is like living among snow capped peaks with clouds wrapped around them and the sun and the moon shining brightly. Below tall trees are swayed by the howling winds and beneath them is a thundering waterfall.

From our point of view, we may appreciate this desolation if we are an occasional tourist who photographs it or a mountain climber trying to climb the mountain top but we do not really want to live in those places. It's no fun. It is terrifying, terrible." ~ Chogyam Trungpa in "The Myth of Freedom and the Way of Meditation

This is what Jesus Christ meant when he said "Where I am going I you can not follow but later you will follow". John 13:36 KJV

It is what St. John of the Cross wrote about: The dark night of the soul.

In that place, there is no one to catch you if you fall.

You are all alone and you have to deal with it. There is a natural tendency to want to take others with you. The ego wants this because it is another way of validating yourself.

You want to go back, escape, but there is no escape.

The stages of awakening follows if at first you don't go insane.

First, dealing with boredom, relating with the neurosis of your mind and befriending your ego instead of fighting it.

The way of the Bodhisattva and then the way of the warrior.

Then upon surrendering, seeing the universe dance at your feet, bliss.

One can, and some do, stay in this stage for eons. Sooner or later, one has to deal with aloneness, the inevitable aloneness that comes after the bliss.

This is when one decides to step in to the gateway of the unknown or go back to the way it was and start all over. Another lifetime.

And then, perhaps, one day one can come back and show others The Path. Coming down from the snow peaked mountains is much faster, for now the clouds have parted and the sun illuminates everything and for the first time one sees that it was impossible to fall. One had to experience the fear. It was part of the test.

The Six Kinds of Power

"It began with the forging of the great rings. Three were given to the elves, the wisest and fairest (most just) of all creatures, seven to the dwarf lords, great miners and craftsmen of the mountain' ores and nine...nine rings were gifted to race of men...who above all else desire POWER..." Lord of the Rings

One afternoon, as I was cleaning my spam box I came across an ad and curiously opened it. It was a video about the four kinds of power. It was fascinating in the sense that it only talked about physical power, social power, economic power and spiritual power. It missed or ignored intellectual power, as well as political power. I thought that was odd and then I realized that this was a promotional video. There are probably other kinds of power such as magical power but those I attribute to spiritual power.

Let us talk briefly about these powers.
Physical power is what the martial artists have.
Social power is what the celebrities have.

Economic power is what the wealthy people have. This is the only one that can be bestowed from one person to another, i.e. inheritance money.

Political power is what the elected officials have.

Intellectual power is what the scientists and artists have, and lastly,

Spiritual power is what the magicians/shamans have, and at the highest degree what the sages of the past, and realized beings have.

Except for the last one, all of the other powers overlap to some degree and one can be used to get others.

The last one encompasses them all, the main difference being those endowed with spiritual power can, at will, and in full knowing, take any of the earlier powers if they choose to do so. As in all cases, there are varying degrees.

For the last one, there is an infinite range of degrees.

I am thinking of the sages of the past. One of the most famous lines in a Zen book was the fact that the old Zen Masters, instead of being enfeebled by age were empowered by it.

To acquire any of the six powers one requires discipline. The question then is "What would you give to acquire your chosen power?"

The koan in Wumenguan entitled "The wild fox" asks this question: "Is a greatly cultivated man also subject to causality? The correct answer is : He is not blind to causality"

This was what Jesus Christ meant when he said "To be in the world but not of it."

Note: If you want economic power then you should be able to say yes to what Milton in the Devil's Advocate asked Kevin, the lawyer:

"Can you summon your talent at will? Can you deliver on a deadline? Can you sleep at night?"

Lastly, there is nothing wrong with trying to develop/acquire any of these powers. That is what free will is about. Just remember that with privilege always comes responsibility.

You define what those are.

Discipline is the Only Way

According to the Merriam-Webster dictionary online, discipline means the following:
dis·ci·pline
Pronunciation: \'di-s?-pl?n\
Function: noun
Etymology: Middle English, from Anglo-French & Latin; Anglo-French, from Latin disciplina teaching, learning, from discipulus pupil
Date: 13th century
1: punishment
2 obsolete : instruction
3: a field of study
4: training that corrects, molds, or perfects the mental faculties or moral character
5 a: control gained by enforcing obedience or order b: orderly or prescribed conduct or pattern of behavior c: self-control
6: a rule or system of rules governing conduct or activity

A samurai practices kendo, every day. A monk sits in meditation every day. A pious person prays every day. A world class athlete trains everyday for an event one year ahead.

Even the Buddha sat in meditation after realizing enlightenment.

There is value in repetitive tasks. It quiets the mind of chatter. Being able to do something repetitively involves the discipline to do it day after day.

Chogyam Trungpa once said, in order to go to depths of meditation, one has to first be able to sit and relate to the boredom and the simplicity of meditation.

Just follow your breath. When one is able to relate to the boredom then all of the last 4 definitions of discipline are fulfilled.

The progression of the path to freedom goes : From discipline, knowledge, from knowledge, understanding, from understanding, awareness, from awareness, detachment, from detachment, freedom.

or put it another way

From discipline, knowledge, from knowledge, wisdom, from wisdom, discriminating awareness, from discriminating awareness, ruthless compassion from ruthless compassion, freedom.

Epilogue

Man, 2009
Ceasing from Becoming

A single flash of insight
Lifetimes of darkness gone
Unshackled free from thought,
or traces of thought
All at once, see Here and Now.
Past and future gone,
No more becoming
Forever free, at last.
Man lives. Still.
Yet, Still
Dancing the Dance of Illusion

About the Author

Melinda was born, raised, and educated in the Philippines, and came to the USA to pursue post graduate education.

After obtaining her Masters and Ph.D. degrees, and after doing Postdoctoral research, she worked as a Professor of Chemistry for several years.

Both as a student and as a professor, Melinda was a recipient of many scholarships/awards/grants and in addition Melinda was mentored by many generous men and women during her career.

As a professor she has mentored students who have gone on to careers in the medical fields, chemistry and other science related fields as well as business and technology.

Melinda published articles in peer reviewed scientific journals before leaving the academia.

In 2007, Melinda published a book/journal "My Journey to an Integrated Life, a Journal of Self Discovery."

Melinda also published several articles in online magazines.

In her own journey, Melinda has seen the never ending circle of life.

Sometimes we give, sometimes we receive, sometimes we comfort others, sometimes we are comforted.

About the Author

Melinda recognizes that while it is true that there is suffering in this world, there is also the beautiful human heart which sees that in every human interaction, be it with nature or with other human beings, there is hope and there is love.

A fearless heart embraces all of it: The suffering and the alleviation of suffering both our own and that of others. In the pursuit of our own humanity, we find that we are all inextricably, intimately and infinitely connected with each other.

We only have to pay attention to discover our fearless hearts.

Melinda currently serves as President of Fearless Hearts Foundation. She can be reached at email : info@fearlessheartsfoundation.org

For more information on Fearless Hearts Foundation, please visit the website at www.fearlessheartsfoundation.org

Fearless Hearts Foundation publishes a monthly newsletter,
InfiniSynechis.

To learn more, please visit our website and go to Foundation News and Updates.

https://fearlessheartsfoundation.org/foundation-news-and-updates

About the Author

Creed of the Fearless Hearts

I would be true, for there are those who trust me; I would be pure, for there are those who care; I would be strong, for there is much to suffer; I would be brave, for there is much to dare; I would be friend of all-the foe, the friendless; I would be giving, and forget the gift; I would be humble, for I know my weakness; I would look up, and laugh, and love and lift. I would be faithful through each passing moment. I would be constantly in touch with God; I would be strong to follow where I lead me; I would have faith to keep the path Christ trod. Who is so low that I am not his brother? Who is so high that I've no path to him? Who is so poor? I can not feel his hunger? Who is so rich I may not pity him? Who is so hurt I can not know his heartache? Who sings for joy my heart may never share? Who in God's heav'n has passed beyond my vision? Who to hell's depths where I may never fare? May None, then, call me for understanding. May none, then, turn to me for help in pain, and drain alone his bitter cup of sorrow, or find he knocks upon my heart in vain.

Adapted from
My Creed and Other Poems, - Howard Arnold
Walter, 1912

About the Author

Books by the same author:

My Journey to an Integrated Life, a Journal of Self
Discovery
First Edition
ISBN 978-0-9796507-0-3

Short Stories, Essays and Exercises on the Path to
Self Discovery
Volume I
ISBN 978-0-9796507-1-0

My Journey to an Integrated Life, a Journal of Self
Discovery
Second Edition
ISBN 978-0-9796507-2-7

www.ingramcontent.com/pod-product-compliance
Lightning Source LLC
Chambersburg PA
CBHW031404180326
41458CB00043B/6609/J